Highlights of

CHURCH
HISTORY

By Howard F. Vos

MOODY PRESS
CHICAGO

CONTENTS

Chapter I

BEGINNINGS

THE PASSOVER SEASON was ended. The crowds that had gathered for the occasion dispersed and Jerusalem returned to normal. Some were puzzled by the unusual circumstances surrounding the crucifixion of a certain Jesus of Nazareth who appeared to be a revolutionist—for he had tried to set up a kingdom of his own. A rumor had spread concerning his resurrection from the dead, but certainly that was impossible, they thought. Had not the soldiers who guarded his tomb reported the theft of his body by his followers? That was sufficient explanation for most. Another Galilean rabble rouser had come to the end of his rope.

One hundred and twenty of His followers gathered in an upper room knew different. Having seen and talked with the risen Lord, they awaited at His command the coming of the Holy Spirit. On the Day of Pentecost (fifty days after the crucifixion and ten days after the ascension) they were rewarded. A sound as of a rushing wind filled the house. On each of the group lighted what appeared to be a tongue of flame. Immediately they were filled with the Spirit and began to speak in other tongues. Rapidly word of this phenomenon spread among Jews gathered for the Feast of Pentecost, and a crowd came rushing to investigate. Upon arrival, they all heard the message of truth in their own language. Some marveled. Others accused the Disciples of being intoxicated. This was a foolish assertion because drunkenness would only produce gibberish, not intelligible conversation in another language.

Besides it was early in the day—too early for such a large group to be drunk. At this point Peter arose and addressed the throng. He pointed out that this remarkable phenomenon was a result of the Holy Spirit's ministry among them. Then he preached Christ: His death, resurrection, and ascension and the present necessity of receiving Him by faith as Saviour and being baptized in His name. The Holy Spirit so wrought that three thousand believed on that memorable day.

Thus the Church was born.[1] And wonderful was the experience of believers during succeeding days. They held the true doctrine, were faithful in prayer, partook frequently of the Lord's Supper, enjoyed each other's fellowship, were in one accord, and lived joyous lives. Those who met them were strangely moved and awed; many believed *daily* (Acts 2:42-47). Soon the number of Church members swelled to about 5,000 men; in addition there were probably women and children (Acts 4:4).

But believers were not merely to enjoy a state of ecstasy. They were made aware of this by persecution which the Temple priests initiated (Acts 4). Accepting the Lord was a serious business; it involved suffering for His sake. Were they any better than He? The world hated Him; it would hate His followers also (John 15:18-19). Persecution came with increasing frequency and intensity. First there was warning, then beating, then murder. Stephen was the first Christian martyr (Acts 7:54-60).

---

[1] The writer recognizes that not all agree the Church originated at Pentecost. But note that one becomes a member of the Church by means of the baptism of the Holy Spirit, which act joins him to the mystical body of Christ (I Cor. 12:13 ff.). The baptism of the Holy Spirit was future in the Gospels (Matt. 3:11; Mark 1:8; Luke 3:16; John 1:33; cf. Matt. 16:18) and in Acts 1:5. It is past in Acts 11:15-16. Where else could one logically begin the baptism than at Pentecost? If the beginning of the baptism of the Holy Spirit, by which one becomes a member of the Church, occurs at Pentecost, then the Church must begin there.

But persecution had the opposite of the desired effect. Members of the Jerusalem Church were scattered all over Judea and Samaria, preaching as they went. Philip went to Samaria to minister and witnessed a wonderful spiritual awakening there. The fulfillment of our Lord's commission to preach in Jerusalem, Judea, Samaria, and the uttermost part of the earth (Acts 1:8) was being realized.

At this point a certain Saul of Tarsus, a devout Pharisee who had participated in the persecution of Christians and had been present at the stoning of Stephen, became a prominent persecutor of Christians. To stamp out the hated sect, he even determined to move against believers at Damascus. On the way north he was stopped dead in his tracks by the Lord he opposed (Acts 9). Traveling on to Damascus, Paul was filled with the Holy Spirit and received water baptism there. After that he spent three years in Arabia and then returned to his home town. Fourteen years later Paul returned to Jerusalem with Barnabas, who won the Apostles' approval for Paul (Gal. 1:16-21). Meanwhile the Palestinian Church continued to grow, and Peter introduced the Gospel to the Gentiles of Cornelius' household in Caesarea (Acts 10). The Church in Syria mushroomed too, and Christians were first called Christians in Antioch of Syria.

When Barnabas and Paul came to Antioch from Jerusalem, the Lord revealed to the Church that He wanted them to engage in missionary activity. The pair departed, with the blessing of the whole Church, to minister to Jews and Gentiles in the regions beyond. They traveled and preached in Cyprus and Asia Minor (modern Turkey) and returned to Antioch. When they arrived, a question of the relationship of Jew and Gentile in the Church and to the Law arose. The issue was referred to the Jerusalem Church; Paul and Barnabas and others were sent there to present the case. The decision of the great Council of

Jerusalem (49 or 50 A.D.) is significant: "For it seemed good to the Holy Spirit, and to us, to lay upon you no greater burden than these necessary things; That ye abstain from meats offered to idols, and from blood, and from things strangled, and from fornication: from which if ye keep yourselves, ye shall do well" (Acts 15:28-29). Under the guidance of the Holy Spirit, the Council decided that the Law, which had been an impossible burden for the Jew, should not be required of Gentiles.

On Paul's second missionary journey he was accompanied by Silas. The two again visited churches in Asia Minor and then, arrested by the man from Macedonia (Acts 16:9), they crossed over into Greece, where they established churches at Philippi, Thessalonica, Berea, and Corinth. At Corinth Paul remained for about eighteen months in successful evangelization work. During this journey he also preached his famous sermon on Mars Hill (Acts 17). On his third journey, Paul again called on the believers in Eastern Asia Minor. Traveling westward, he stopped at Ephesus for about three years, where he carried the Gospel banner to victory over the forces of Diana. Revisiting the churches in Greece, he returned to Jerusalem, where he was apprehended by the leaders of the Jews and imprisoned. At length, appealing to Caesar, he was taken to Rome for trial. There he was imprisoned for two years (apparently under a sort of house arrest, Acts 28:30), and there he enjoyed a fairly successful ministry to the many who had access to him. Tradition has it that Paul was released from prison and engaged in a fourth missionary journey, when he went to Spain and possibly southern France. He also seems to have gone to Crete, in addition to visiting some churches already established.

During the first century the other Apostles were active. Several apparently evangelized areas not already mentioned. Tradition has it that Bartholomew preached in Armenia; Thomas in Parthia, Persia, and India; Matthew in Ethiopia; James the Less in Egypt; Jude in Assyria and Persia; and Mark (not one of the Apostles but closely related to them) in Alexandria. If the Babylon from which Peter wrote (I Peter 5:13) was Babylon on the Euphrates instead of a symbolical representation of Rome, then Babylonia was also evangelized during the first century. If there is any truth in these traditions concerning the Apostles and other early Church leaders, the Gospel, through these men and their converts, penetrated to most of the more important inhabited areas of Europe, Asia, and Africa by the end of the first century.[2] In a real sense then the pattern of evangelism laid out in Acts 1:8 was realized: "But ye shall receive power, after that the Holy Spirit is come upon you: and ye shall be witnesses unto me both in Jerusalem, and in Judea, and in Samaria, and unto the uttermost part of the earth."

---

[2] If India was evangelized during the first century, it is entirely reasonable to suppose that believers also reached China with the Christian message. Moreover, there is evidence that the Gospel reached Britain in the first century. On the general question of the spread of the Gospel over the Empire, remember that a large number of lands was represented at Pentecost: Parthia, Media, Elam, Mesopotamia, Cappadocia, Pontus, Asia, Phrygia, Pamphylia, Egypt, Libya, Crete, Arabia and Rome (Acts 2:9-11). Certainly these converts would witness of Christ upon return to their homelands. Also, Paul and others ministered in cities having a large percentage of transient persons—Corinth, Ephesus, Antioch, etc.

Chapter II

THE FATHERS

As the apostles passed from the scene, other leaders arose in the Church to take their place. These leaders, generally bishops, are called fathers because of the esteem in which they were held by loyal church members. In fact, the term *father* has come to serve as a designation for early church leaders during the period A.D. 90 to about 460.

The men who led the Church during these centuries are frequently divided into four groups: the Apostolic Fathers (90–150); the Apologists (130–180); the Polemicists (180–225); and the Scientific Theologians (225–460). Sometimes they are classified as the Apostolic Fathers (second century); the Ante-Nicene Fathers (second and third centuries); the Nicene Fathers (fourth century); and the Post-Nicene Fathers (fifth century; sometimes to Gregory the Great in 590). The first group is characterized by edification, the second by defense against attacks of Roman officialdom, the third by attacks against heresy within the Church, and the fourth by a scientific study of theology in an effort to apply to theological investigation philosophical modes of thought then current.

THE APOSTOLIC FATHERS

While the Apostle John was writing Revelation on the Isle of Patmos or at Ephesus, Clement served as leading elder in the church at Rome. In this capacity he assumed responsibility for answering an appeal (as did Paul a half century earlier; cf. I Cor. 7:1 ff.) from the Church at Corinth for advice on how to quell a disturbance there. He sent a letter urging a demonstration of Christian graces in daily relationships and obedience to the elders and deacons against whom some were rebelling. Because this is the earliest extra-Biblical Christian writing, it has attained a place of prominence among the writings of the Apostolic Fathers. About a half century later, another Roman, Hermas, wrote a work known as the *Shepherd of Hermas.* In it he records five visions which serve as the basis of commands concerning the rooting out of evils existent in the church of his day. In the description of these evils the writer gives a picture of the level of Christian living about A.D. 150. It is far from high. The book of *Second Clement* was probably written about the same time as the *Shepherd* and was not, therefore, authored by Clement of Rome. Like *First Clement,* it was, however, addressed to the Corinthians. The message of *Second Clement* emphasized practical Christian living and a sound view of Christ.

A Syrian Apostolic Father was Ignatius, bishop of Antioch. About 110 he was apprehended by Roman authorities because of his Christian profession and sent to Rome for martyrdom. Along the way he wrote letters to various churches. These seven letters were designed to promote unity in the churches addressed. Unity was to be accomplished on the one hand by rooting out heresies denying the full divine-human personality of Christ, and on the other hand by the subjection of leaders in local congregations to a ruling bishop. Thus impetus was given to the power of bishops, but only over a local congregation.

In Asia Minor (modern Turkey) two Fathers were active: Polycarp and Papias. Polycarp, bishop of Smyrna, is particularly interesting to the modern Christian because he was a disciple of the Apostle John. One of his letters remains addressed to the Philippians. As one would expect from a disciple of John, Polycarp emphasized in his letter faith in Christ and the necessary outworking of that faith in daily living. Unlike Ignatius, his concerns do not involve church organization and discipline. Papias, bishop of Hierapolis in Phrygia, wrote about the middle of the second century, some thirty-five years after Polycarp. His *Interpretations of the Sayings (Oracles) of the Lord* is now lost, but portions survive in the writings of Irenaeus and Eusebius. These portions deal with the life and teachings of Christ and attempt to preserve information obtained from those who had known Christ. They are especially interesting for their historical references, such as the statement that Mark got the information for his Gospel from Peter.

Works assigned to the period of the Apostolic Fathers also originated in North Africa. Barnabas is generally considered to have been written in Alexandria—probably somewhere between A.D. 70 and 120. Like much of the other literature of Alexandria his epistle is quite allegorical in nature, engaging in gross typology and numerology. The basic problem of the epistle concerns the necessity of a Christian's keeping the law. He holds that such was not necessary; the work of Christ was sufficient. He becomes so anti-Judaic as almost to deny a historical connection between Judaism and Christianity. The *Didache* or *Teachings of the Twelve* is also believed to have originated in Alexandria, probably during the first decades of the second century. A church manual, divided into three parts, the *Didache* treats Christian ethics, liturgical and disciplinary matters, and the need for a life of preparedness in view of the return of Christ.

The Apostolic Fathers must be evaluated in accordance

with their apparent purpose: to exhort and edify the Church. Sometimes they are criticized by evangelicals because they do not seem to grasp the New Testament concept of salvation by faith or because they seem to neglect certain doctrines. It should be remembered, however, that if one's purpose is to exhort to a higher plane of Christian living, he may make rather obscure allusions to the means by which one becomes a Christian. Moreover, informal utterances of pious faith are not designed to provide completeness of theological treatment and should not be judged by the same criteria as a systematic theology. Admittedly, however, the Apostolic Fathers do in some instances seem to assign a rather significant place to baptism as a medium of forgiveness of sin. Martyrdom and celibacy are also thought to have special sin-atoning power. On the whole, the Apostolic Fathers picture a Church still throbbing with missionary zeal, a Church in which individual responsibility is still everywhere recognized, and a Church in which hierarchal organization is at a minimum.

THE APOLOGISTS

The approach and purpose of the Apologists was entirely different from that of the Apostolic Fathers. The Apologists sought to win legal recognition for Christianity and to defend it against certain charges leveled against it by the pagan populace. In constructing this defense,[1] the Apologists wrote in a more philosophical vein than the Apostolic Fathers. A generation of Christians from a higher social class and with more extensive education had arisen.

---

[1] Apology in its basic meaning signifies *defense;* it is so used by the Apologists. The fact that the word has taken on the connotation of *making excuse* should not confuse the reader.

In seeking to win a place in the sun for Christianity, the Apologists tried on the one hand to demonstrate the superiority of the Hebrew Christian tradition over paganism, and on the other to defend Christianity against certain charges. This superiority was both temporal and spiritual. Justin Martyr claimed that Moses wrote the Pentateuch long before the Trojan War (c. 1200 B.C.), thus antedating Greek history, to say nothing of Roman. And he and other Apologists made much of fulfillment of prophecy in an attempt to show that Christianity was not something new but merely a continuation or culmination of the ancient Hebrew faith. As to spiritual superiority of Christianity over paganism, the Apologists claimed that noble pagans had obtained their high ideals from God or Moses.

Charges against which Apologists defended Christianity were atheism, cannibalism, immorality, and anti-social action. The first charge arose because Christians refused to worship the emperor or the Graeco-Roman gods; the second because of a misunderstanding of the celebration of the Lord's Supper; the third because religious services generally had to be conducted in secret or after dark and because Christians displayed great love for each other; and the last because Christians found it necessary to retire from much public life, since most aspects of human existence were in some way connected with worship of the gods.

In their effort to win recognition from the State for their faith, the Apologists generally took a philosophical approach. It was only natural that they should do so because on the one hand they were trying to reason out the case for Christianity with their opponents, and because on the other hand they often wrote to men who were themselves greatly interested in philosophy. (Note, for instance, that the Emperor Marcus Aurelius was a Stoic philosopher. Several apologies were addressed to him.) Because of their philosophical orientation, the Apologists have been accused of undue surrender to the world view of heathenism. Even their teachings about Jesus Christ appear in the form of the Logos doctrine. To the Philosophers, the Logos was an impersonal controlling and developing principle of the universe. But John in chapter 1 of his Gospel had also used the term *Logos* to describe Christ, without any sacrifice of His deity or the value of His atoning work. And the Apologists on most points seem to have upheld the New Testament concept of Jesus Christ, though it must be admitted that such writers as Justin sometimes described Christ as a being of inferior rank to the Father. The very fact that the Apologists placed such great stress on the Logos demonstrates that their theology was Christ-centered. Moreover, while the practice might involve dangers, it is neither wrong nor undesirable to make one's message intelligible to one's age.

Probably the most dramatic and therefore the best known of the Apologists was Justin Martyr. Certainly he was a great literary defender of the faith. Born about A.D. 100 in a small town in Samaria, Justin early became well acquainted with various philosophical systems. But his great knowledge of these philosophies also led him to a realization of their inadequacies. At this point of disillusionment and searching, an old Christian came into Justin Martyr's life and showed him the way of faith in Christ. Thereafter the converted philosopher became a Christian philosopher, presenting the Christian message in philosophical terms. He wrote two apologies to the Emperor Antoninus Pius and his adopted son, Marcus Aurelius, and a dialogue with Trypho the Jew. In the apologies he sought to defend Christianity against the charges of atheism and immorality, to demonstrate that Christians

were loyal citizens (Christ's kingdom was not of this
world; so the Empire had no reason to fear insurrection),
and to prove that the truth was taught by Christianity
alone. In his dialogue with Trypho, Justin tried to show
that Jesus was the Messiah. On his second stay in Rome,
Justin engaged in a public debate with a philosopher by
the name of Crescens. Shortly thereafter (c. 165) he was
martyred by Marcus Aurelius, perhaps at the instigation
of several philosophers close to the Emperor.

One of Justin's converts in Rome was Tatian, a writer
skilled in argumentation. His *Address to the Greeks* was
largely a tirade against paganism, sarcastically ridiculing
almost every pagan practice. In the latter part he argued
that since Christianity was superior to Greek religion and
thought, it deserved to be tolerated. After Justin's martyrdom, Tatian drifted off into the error of Gnosticism.
(For a discussion see Chapter III.) Probably Tatian is
best known for his *Diatessaron,* the earliest harmony of
the Gospels, composed about A.D. 160–170. Another
writer of note sometimes classified among the Apologists
was Tertullian. Born in Carthage about 160, he later
moved to Rome where he became a lawyer and was sub-
sequently won to Christianity. His *Apologeticus,* addressed
to the Roman governor of Carthage, refuted the common
charges leveled against Christians, demonstrated their
loyalty to the Empire, and showed that persecution of
Christians was foolish anyway because they multiplied
whenever persecuted. About 200 Tertullian became en-
meshed in the error of Montanism. (For a discussion see
Chapter III.) While these three were the more important
of the Apologists, fragmentary or fairly complete writings
of at least a half dozen others exist. A discussion of those
writers is not significant for the present study, however.

THE POLEMICISTS

As the Christian movement grew older, errors arose within its ranks—errors which called forth defenders of the faith and which by reaction led to the development of Christian doctrine and the formulation of a New Testament canon. It is significant that in refuting error the Polemicists appealed extensively to New Testament books as the source of true doctrine. Thus they gave impetus to the later official pronouncements on the contents of the New Testament canon. The work of the Polemicists gave rise also to the concept of an orthodox catholic church opposed to heresy. Since a large part of the next chapter is devoted to a definition of these errors, note is made here only of the chief attackers of them.

While most of the Apologists lived in the East, most of the Polemicists lived in the West. Earliest of these was Irenaeus who wrote his five books *Against Heresies* about 185 at Lyons, France. Primarily aimed against the philosophical error of Gnosticism, these books may be characterized as follows: Book I—a historical sketch of Gnostic sects presented in conjunction with a statement of Christian faith; Book II—a philosophical critique of Gnosticism; Book III—a scriptural critique of Gnosticism; Book IV—answers to Gnosticism from the words of Christ; Book V—a vindication of the resurrection against Gnostic arguments.

Covering much the same ground as Irenaeus, Hippolytus also attacked Gnosticism, as well as other errors, in his *Refutation of All Heresies* (written about 200). While Hippolytus may have borrowed from Irenaeus, he significantly supplements the work of the latter. Hippolytus came into conflict with the dominant party in Rome because he criticized them for disciplinary laxness and doctrinal unsoundness. In particular, he linked Callixtus, an important pastor, with Noetianism and Sabellianism—early forms of Unitarianism.

In Carthage lived two other western Polemicists: Tertullian and Cyprian. Tertullian might be classified with the Apologists if one emphasizes his *Apologeticus* or as a scientific theologian if one emphasizes his *De Anima* (concerning the origin of the soul). In fact, he is commonly regarded as the founder of Latin theology. But he is classified here because of his intensely passionate opposition to paganism, Judaism, early forms of Unitarianism, and Gnosticism. It has been said that he did more to overthrow Gnosticism than any other. While Tertullian lapsed into the Montanistic error (involving a perversion of the doctrine of the Holy Spirit), he renewed fellowship with the Church before his death. Tertullian's ministry was carried on during the first decades of the third century.

Cyprian (martyred in 258) in his polemic activity is known for his opposition to Novatianism. Novatus (Novatian) held that those who lapsed during persecution could not be pronounced forgiven by the Church and restored to its fellowship; forgiveness must be left to God alone. It was not Novatus' severity of discipline but his denial that the Church had the right to grant absolution that caused his excommunication. The Church had become conscious of her catholicity and unity by this time, and those who would not submit to divinely appointed bishops were regarded as heretics. In line with this common attitude, Cyprian, Bishop of Carthage, felt duty bound to condemn Novatus.

Sometimes leaders of the School of Alexandria are listed among the Polemicists. Clement's *Protrepticus* is an apologetic missionary document written to demonstrate the superiority of Christianity to paganism. Origen wrote his *Against Celsus* to answer certain charges against

Christianity. But it is the opinion of the writer that these men are more properly classified among the scientific theologians.

THE SCIENTIFIC THEOLOGIANS

As has been noted already, the scientific theologians sought to apply to theological investigation modes of thought then current. Moreover, they tried to develop scientific methods of Biblical interpretation and textual criticism. The classification of these writers falls roughly into three groups. Those of the West (Jerome, Ambrose, Augustine) tended to emphasize the authority of the Church and its tradition. Writers living in Alexandria (Pantaenus, Clement, Origen) were the most speculative in approach. Those ministering in Asia Minor and Syria (Theodore of Mopsuestia, John Chrysostom, *et al.*) took a generally literal approach to Biblical study.

Earliest of the leaders of the school in Alexandria for converts from paganism and children of believers was Pantaenus, who held the reins of authority until 200. Since the writings of Pantaenus no longer exist (or have not yet been discovered), it is necessary to move along to a discussion of his more famous successors. Associated with Pantaenus from 190, Clement headed the school of Alexandria from 200 to 202, when he was forced by persecution to leave the city. His writings include *Address to the Greeks, The Tutor, The Miscellanies,* and the *Outlines of Scripture Interpretation.* The first was designed to win converts from heathenism, the second to provide simple instruction for new converts and the young, the third to show the superiority of Christianity to pagan philosophy, and the last to provide commentaries on various scriptural passages—partly in answer to heretical interpretations. In the writings of Clement, the influence of Greek philosophy is prominent, especially that of

Plato; but the Bible also has a place of importance. He
seeks to synthesize Christianity and Greek philosophy
and is significant in Church history as being the first to
present Christianity in the forms of secular literature for
the Christian community.

Most famous of the Alexandrian writers was Origen,
who led the school from 202 to 232. He brought to
scientific formulation the allegorical interpretation of
Scripture. The germs of this approach may be seen in
Philo of Alexandria, a contemporary of Christ who sought
to find a reconciliation between Greek Philosophy and
Jewish thought by searching for hidden meanings in the
Old Testament. Christian writers after him had employed
the Allegorical method, but Origen receives the credit
for the full development of the approach. Simply described, it holds that the literal meaning of Scripture
conceals a deeper meaning available only to the mature
believer. The hidden meaning which he found sometimes
bore little or no relationship to the literal. This conceal-
ing of truth by God under the guise of commonly under-
stood words was designed to prevent pearls from being
cast before swine.

Origen's works number in the thousands, involving
critical, apologetic, dogmatic, and practical treatises. His
commentaries deal with almost the whole Bible. While
they are helpful at points, their value is restricted by his
allegorisms. Highly significant are his critical or textual
studies: the *Hexapla* and *Tetrapla*. The former has several Hebrew and Greek versions arranged in parallel
columns. The latter contains the four Greek versions of
the *Hexapla*. While only fragments of these two critical
works remain, they are of great value.

While Origen made some positive contributions to
the theology of the Church, he is more commonly known
for views which did not receive general acceptance.

For instance, he taught that the souls of men existed as fallen spirits before the birth of the individual; that accounted for man's sinful nature. Second, he held that in His atonement Christ paid a ransom to Satan, by whom all were enslaved in the bondage of sin. Third, he believed that the rejected, who go to Hell at death, would experience there a purifying fire which ultimately would cleanse even the wicked; all would ultimately reach the state of bliss.

One of the greatest of the Western Fathers was Jerome (341–420). Born in Eastern Europe, he was converted in Rome. Except for a few scattered years in Rome, he spent most of his life in the East. Settling in a monastery at Bethlehem in 386 he began his influential writing ministry. By means of extensive correspondence and dramatic lives of early ascetics, he did much to promote asceticism and celibacy. As a writer against heresies, Jerome was primarily the interpreter of accepted Church dogma; he was not original. His commentaries on the Bible are extensive but are unequal in value. Allegorism is utilized, according to his own admission, when he was unable to discover the literal meaning. Jerome ranks first among early exegetes. He was careful about his sources of information. He knew and used extensively early manuscripts of the Bible no longer extant. Operating on the principle that only the original text of Scripture is free from error, he engaged in considerable manuscript study in order to determine what, among variant readings, should be considered the original and true text. Out of these efforts came the work for which he is best known: the Vulgate, a translation of the Bible into Latin. Jerome also tried to bring Eusebius' *Ecclesiastical History* [2] up to date by re-

---

[2] Eusebius of Caesarea lived about 260–341 and composed a Church history which serves as a mine of information about the early Church. While it is not a great literary work nor a well

cording events for the years 325–378.

Ambrose, Bishop of Milan (374–397) was another of the most illustrious fathers of the Western Church. Because his writings represent an official witness to the teachings of the Roman Church in his own time and earlier centuries, they have been constantly appealed to by popes, councils, and theologians. Commentaries on Scripture constitute more than half of his writings. In these commentaries Ambrose employs the allegorico-mystical method of interpretation: he admits a literal sense but seeks everywhere a deeper mystic meaning that he converts into practical instruction for Christian life. Ambrose is also known for his contributions in the field of music. But apparently tradition has been too kind to him. So far no documents have been brought to light to prove he composed anything but the melodies to most of his hymns. And while a large number of hymns have been attributed to him, less than twenty can be attributed to him with certainty.

St. Augustine, Bishop of Hippo in North Africa, stands pre-eminent among theologians of all time. His influence upon all faiths has been significant. His emphasis on a personal experience of the grace of God as necessary to salvation has caused him to be accepted as a forerunner of the Reformation by Protestants. His emphasis on the Church, her creed, and sacraments has appealed to Romanists. His teaching that the millennium referred to the period between Christ's first and second comings, during which time the Church would conquer the world, has contributed greatly to amillennial and postmillennial theologies of past and present. Augustine's teaching that man

balanced work (the writer's meager knowledge of Latin prevented him from knowing much about the Western Church), the *Ecclesiastical History* does provide a great deal of information that otherwise would be lost to us. His testimony concerning the canon is particularly valuable.

is totally depraved profoundly influenced Calvinistic theology. And such an outstanding American historian as Perry Miller makes the claim in his *New England Mind* that the Puritans were even more Augustinian than Calvinistic in their theology. Augustine's views on the nature of man and his salvation are described more at length in Chapter IV.

Augustine (354–430) came from a respectable but not a rich family. His life, a journey through periods of immorality, entanglement in appealing philosophies and heresies of the day, and spiritual crisis, to the achievement of moral and spiritual victory is one of the best-known biographies of all time. The account, recorded in his *Confessions,* has been read by millions. While the *Confessions* is Augustine's moral biography, his *Revisions* is his intellectual biography, describing the changes in his thought over the years. Most important of his theological works is his *Concerning the Trinity; Concerning Christian Doctrine* is the most important of his exegetical works. His philosophy of history, the first to be developed, is found in his *City of God.* In it, he traces the development of the city of earth and the city of God through Biblical and secular history and shows the destiny of the two cities: the former to eternal punishment and the latter to eternal bliss. He portrays the sovereignty of God in the affairs of men and the ultimate triumph of good over evil, though the reverse is currently often true.

Two of the most important of the scientific theologians in the Eastern Church were Theodore and John Chrysostom. Theodore (350–428) was bishop of Mopsuestia in Cilicia (Asia Minor) for thirty-six years. Among his more important writings were his commentaries on the Psalms, which were almost exclusively grammatico-historical and realistic explanations of the text. This method of interpreting the words of Scripture according to their ordinary grammatical meaning and in the light of their historical background was the prevailing mode of interpretation in the Antiochene school of thought. John Calvin was later to become famous for his contributions to the grammatico-historical method of Biblical interpretation.

John Chrysostom (347–407), the most prominent doctor of the Greek Church, also was important as a representative of the grammatico-historical interpretation of Scripture in opposition to the allegorical and mystical interpretations of Alexandria. While Chrysostom did not exclude all allegorical and mystical elements from scriptural study, he confined them to cases in which he felt the inspired author suggested such a meaning. Chrysostom is also important for the formation of Eastern theology. At the time of the Reformation there were long discussions as to whether he was Protestant or Catholic. He ignored confession to a priest and there is no clear reference in his writings to the primacy of the pope. But he did hold to the real presence in the Eucharist, to the One Church, and to tradition as a valid basis of authority. Chrysostom was for some years Patriarch of Constantinople. Perhaps he is best known for his preaching. The name "Chrysostom," meaning "golden mouthed," was bestowed upon him for his eloquence. Copies of some 650 of his sermons still exist.

A study of the Fathers is very valuable for one interested in the development of Church doctrine and organization. In their lives and teachings we find the seed plot of all that arose later. In germ form appear the dogma of purgatory, transubstantiation, priestly mediation, baptismal regeneration, and the whole sacramental system. They defined the allegorical, mystical, and literal interpretations of Scripture. To them we look for a formulation of the hierarchal system and the importance of the Church as the sphere of salvation. But through them also came the development of the canon and formulation of the great creeds of Christendom, which serve as the basis of most successive teaching concerning the Trinity, the Person of Christ, and the nature of the Holy Spirit. And among them arose great defenders of the faith who answered the persecutors of Christianity and attacked heretics who attempted to destroy the faith from within. It is to the persecutions and perversions of the faith that we now turn.

Chapter III

FOES WITHOUT AND WITHIN

The Persecutions

THE CHRISTIAN MOVEMENT was hardly launched when it faced its first persecutors. Shortly after Pentecost members of the Sanhedrin became greatly disturbed over the success of apostolic preaching and threw Peter and John into prison (Acts 4). Soon thereafter they imprisoned the whole apostolic band (Acts 5). Opposition heightened, resulting in the stoning of Stephen (Acts 7). A few years later, about A.D. 44, Herod Agrippa I slew James the brother of John (Acts 12:2) and imprisoned Peter. So it was with the Jews that persecution of the Church began. The Romans conducted the great organized persecutions of the early Church.

Jewish reasons for persecuting the Church were different from those of the Romans. Many Jewish leaders feared the loss of their position in Judaism if Christianity gained in considerable numbers. Others felt that Christianity was a dangerous perversion of the true faith, a perversion that must be stamped out.

Reasons for Roman persecution were much more complex. Christians were politically suspect because they spoke of a kingdom with Christ as its ruler. Statements concerning such a kingdom were taken by materialistically minded Romans to be an indication of a plan for overthrow of the Empire. Moreover, there was a union of religion and state in ancient Rome; so refusal to worship the goddess Roma or the divine emperor constituted treason. And no government has ever dealt lightly with treason. Christians were socially ostracized because they came, especially in the early days, from the lowest classes of society and because as good Christians they could not participate in much of the public life of their time. For instance, as civil servants they might be required to participate in ceremonies in honor of the divine Caesar. Even engaging in sporting and theatrical events involved one in a certain amount of homage to the gods. And the fact that Christians proclaimed the equality of all men before God put them in direct opposition to the generally accepted institution of slavery.

There were also economic reasons for the persecution of Christians. Priests, idol makers, and other vested religious interests could hardly look on disinterestedly while their incomes dwindled and their very livelihood stood in jeopardy. Since leaders of the old religions held important positions in society, they could easily stir up mob opposition to Christianity. The success of Demetrius and the other idol makers of Ephesus in this regard is a case in point (Acts 19). Christians were also made the scapegoat for great calamities, such as famine, earthquakes and pestilence—which were sometimes regarded as punishment meted out because people had forsaken the Graeco-Roman gods.

Religiously, Christianity suffered because it was exclusivistic, not tolerant like other faiths of the Empire. In fact, it was aggressive in trying to win adherents from other faiths. And because Christians had to hold religious observances in secret, it was easy for all sorts of rumors to circulate about them. Some saw in their love for each other an evidence of licentiousness. Others interpreted their statements used in connection with the communion

service concerning eating the body and drinking the blood
of Christ to refer to cannibalism.

The event which sparked official persecutions, however, was the fire of Rome, July of A.D. 64. That holocaust,
which lasted for six days and seven nights and gutted ten
of the fourteen districts of the city, brought untold suffering to the population of some 2,000,000. Whether or not
Nero started the fire and then sought to shift the blame
to Christians need not concern us here; the fact is
he blamed them for it. The penalty suffered by many of
the supposed incendiaries was burning at the stake at
night to light the public gardens. Some were thrown to
wild beasts or mad dogs. Paul suffered martyrdom at the
hands of Nero; Peter is said to have suffered the same
fate. The Neronian persecution is important because it
established the principle and the manner of persecuting
Christians.

The second persecution broke out about A.D. 90, during the reign of Domitian. Actually, it was originally
directed against Jews who refused to pay a tax to Jupiter
Capitolinus. Being associated with Judaism still, Christians also suffered during this persecution. Domitian generally enforced emperor worship. Upon refusal to participate, Christians were charged with treason. Some were
martyred, some dispossessed of property, and others banished. It was at this time that the Apostle John was exiled
to the Isle of Patmos, where he received the vision of
the Revelation.

Definite imperial policy concerning persecution was not
developed until early in the second century. Pliny the
Younger, a Roman lawyer, served as governor of the
provinces of Bithynia and Pontus in Asia Minor 111–113.
While there, he faced a great defection from paganism
and corresponding growth of the Christian movement. He
felt obligated to deal with this situation and concluded

that those brought before him for trial should be asked three times if they were Christians, each time the question being accompanied with threats. If they persisted in their faith after the third repetition of the question, they were to be led out and executed. Uncertain of the rightness of his procedure, Pliny wrote to the Emperor, Trajan, for advice. Trajan replied that Christians were not to be sought out; but if reported and convicted they were to be punished, unless they repented and worshiped the gods. Anonymous information was not to be received against them. Thus an official policy was established. Soon governors throughout the Empire were following the principles Trajan had enunciated. Many were martyred, including the famous Church Father Ignatius, Bishop of Antioch, who was thrown to wild beasts in the Colosseum about 115.

During the reign of Trajan's successor, Hadrian (117–138) the general policy of Trajan was followed, but Christians were persecuted in moderation. When it became common for the mobs at heathen festivals to demand the blood of Christians, Hadrian published an edict against such riots. Christianity made marked progress in numbers, wealth, learning and social influence during his reign. Antoninus Pius (139–161) seems rather to have favored Christians, but he felt he had to uphold the established imperial policy concerning them. So there were many martyrs, including Polycarp, Bishop of Smyrna. It should be remembered, however, that in many instances during his reign, and particularly in the case of Polycarp, local mobs were responsible for much of the persecution that existed.

A new approach to persecution arose during the reign of Marcus Aurelius (161–180). An intolerant Stoic, he had no sympathy with the concept of immortality. The exultation of Christian martyrs he attributed to their desire for theatrical display. Instead of waiting for ac-

cusation to be brought against Christians as Trajan had
done, Marcus Aurelius introduced a spy system designed
to accumulate evidence against them. He put no check
on the riots instituted against Christians. During his reign,
the practice of blaming the occurrence of earthquake,
famine, flood and pestilence on Christians began. Sup-
posedly these calamities befell the populace because they
tolerated Christianity. Persecution under Marcus Aurelius
was cruel and barbarous. Thousands were beheaded or
thrown to wild beasts, including the famous Justin Martyr.

But even the Aurelian persecution was not an organized
empire-wide persecution for the extermination of Christianity. Neither could the efforts of Septimus Severus
(193–211) and Maximus (235–238) be considered an
all-out war on Christianity. Septimus Severus directed his
attack primarily against Egypt and North Africa, and
even there he was especially interested in putting a stop
to proselytizing. Maximus sought to wipe out Christian
leaders in certain areas.

In the middle of the third century the situation changed,
however. Rome celebrated the thousandth anniversary of
her founding and looked back to the "good old days" of
prosperity, stability and unquestioned authority in the
Mediterranean world. How the gods had favored them!
Now the foundations of the economic, political, and social
structure were crumbling. Public calamities such as earthquake and pestilence abounded. Barbarians hovered on the
frontiers. A superstitious populace was easily persuaded
that the gods were angry with them because so many
Christians had left the old faith. The Emperor was con-
vinced that the maintenance of a state religion was necessary for political stability. Moreover, the fact that Christianity had been favored by his predecessor led him to
suspect Christians of disloyalty to himself. Therefore De-
cius (249–51) embarked on a program to exterminate

Christianity. He published an edict in 250 that all Christians must give up their faith or suffer loss of property, torture and death. The persecution was very cruel and empire-wide. Multitudes perished. Valerian, his successor (253–60) was at first friendly to Christianity, but after a number of public calamities was encouraged to resort to severe punishment of Christians to stop the trouble. Many great leaders lost their lives.

From 260 to 303 Christianity enjoyed respite from persecution. Then all fury broke loose. Diocletian determined to restore the sagging fortunes of empire. Among his reforms was the restoration of the old state religion, which he regarded as a necessary tool for the rehabilitation of empire. Christians became public enemies. Though anticipated by sporadic outbreaks, the great persecution began in 303 with orders to destroy all Christian buildings, to imprison bishops and elders, and to torture all Christians. The following year Christians were offered the alternative of renouncing their faith or martyrdom. It soon became obvious that Christianity had come to stay. Limited toleration was granted in 311 and 313. When Constantine became master of the Eastern part of the Empire, the great persecutions ended. Constantine made Christianity a legal religion and favored its development in many ways. But it was not until near the end of the fourth century that Theodosius made Christianity the official religion of the Empire and persecution of paganism began.

Accounts of the deaths of martyrs during the period of the Roman persecutions have been greatly dramatized. Their faith and courage were magnificent, but theirs was the easy way. Much greater suffering was endured by those who lay in their own filth in heavy irons in hot Eastern prisons—with little water or food until they died of disease or starvation. Equally hard was the lot of those sentenced to work the fields and mines. Half naked, underfed, beaten for low production, the damp ground their bed—theirs was a living death. Are American Christians, living behind a plush curtain and enjoying a cushioned prosperity, made of the same stuff as they?

The persecutions had their effects. Usually the good effects are noted. Many were won to Christ through the manner of death of the martyrs. Tertullian is often quoted: "The blood of the martyrs is the seed of the Church." It is frequently noted that the Church was more apt to be pure if one was in danger of his life for naming the name of Jesus; one would not lightly join for social or economic reasons. But the persecutions had their ill effects too. Christians were so busy protecting themselves that there was little opportunity to leave a literary legacy. And a great problem arose in the Church over the question of the lapsed. All did not hold true to the faith. Some buckled under persecution and then later reaffirmed their faith and wished to be reinstated to the fellowship of believers. Some favored restoration and some did not. Many churches split over the question. Also the very matter of martyrdom became warped as to its purpose or benefits. Many came to believe that dying for the faith had some sin-atoning merit.

EARLY HERESIES

It is probably true that one's greatest enemies are always internal. External opposition or difficulty will not ultimately overpower if internal strength is adequate for the test. So it was with the early Church. The persecutions for the most part only brought about the increase of Christians, while the internal errors of the second and third centuries took a great toll of the faithful.

One of the earliest errors was Ebionism. Appearing in

fully developed form in the second century, it was in reality only a continuation of the Judaistic opposition of the Apostle Paul. In his letter to the Galatians he sternly rebuked those who sought salvation through law keeping. But human nature being what it is, men have always been enamored with religious systems that promise salvation by means of good works; and Ebionism was such a system. Ebionism grew up in Palestine and assumed various forms. Some groups seem to have been quite clear on the essentials of salvation but insistent on law-keeping as a way of life. Most, however, appear to have denied the deity of Christ, His virgin birth, and the efficacy of His sufferings. These views they held in an effort to retain a true monotheism. To them Christ was unusual in His strict law observance, and He was rewarded with Messiahship for His legal piety. The Ebionites generally rejected Paul's apostleship and his writings and tended to venerate Peter as the Apostle to the Circumcision. They put much stress on the law in general and on circumcision and sabbath-keeping in particular. Ebionism practically disappeared by the fifth century. It had little if any lasting effect on the Church.

Like Ebionism, Gnosticism seems to have existed in germ form in the days of Paul. For instance, Colossians 2:18 ff. well may have been aimed at this error. Gnosticism was a philosophical system spawned primarily in Egypt and Syria, though it spread to Rome, Asia Minor, Mesopotamia, and Persia. It borrowed elements from Judaism, Christianity, Greek philosophy, and oriental mysticism. Gnostics taught that matter was evil and spirit was good. Therefore they were faced with the problem of how a good God could create an evil world. A system of emanations was their answer. That is, there emanated from God an infinite chain of beings which became increasingly evil. Finally, at the end of the line came the demiurge or evil

God, the Jehovah of the Old Testament, the Creator of
the world and man. The good God took pity on man in
his plight and sent the highest emanation, Christ, to
minister to man's needs. Especially, Christ came as an
emissary of light from the kingdom of light to dispel man's
spiritual darkness. Because matter was evil, the Messiah's
body was considered by some only to be an appearance,
by others to be a mere human body which the Messiah
used from His baptism until His death on the cross.

Gnosticism derived its name from a Greek word for
knowledge, and emphasis in their system was laid on
attaining knowledge of the good God—which would insure
their salvation. Their system was extremely aristocratic.
The true Gnostic, of whom there were few, was born with
a high degree of intuitive knowledge of God. Ordinary
Church members could attain salvation by faith and good
works. But the mass of humanity did not have a chance
at spiritual salvation. Of great value to the true Gnostic
and the average Church member in attaining an experience of God was initiation into the mysteries of marriage to Christ, baptism, and other mystical rites of the
Church. The path of redemption also involved a low
estimate of the flesh. Some punished the body by extreme
asceticism; others gave full rein to the carnal desires of
the flesh, feeling that in such a manner the flesh could
best be destroyed. At death the soul would be released
from its prison of matter and would return to the Pleroma
—a sort of world soul.

Gnosticism as a system was fairly short lived, partly
because of its inherent weaknesses and partly because the
Polemicists were so effective in dealing with it. It left
lasting effects on the Church, however, negatively in pro-
moting asceticism and division of Christians into higher
and lower orders, and positively in causing the Church to

come to a clearer definition of her doctrine and the limits of her canon.

About the middle of the second century there arose in Phrygia (central Asia Minor) the Montanist error, so named for its leader, Montanus. Montanus taught that the end of the world was at hand and that he was introducing the Age of the Holy Spirit in preparation for the end of all things. He asserted that the Paraclete spoke through him and he claimed special revelations. The Montanists in general laid great emphasis on special spiritual gifts and on a strict asceticism (involving fasting, celibacy, strict moral discipline, etc.) in view of the soon coming of the end of the world. Montanism represented a reaction to the deadness and worldliness of the Church, but its good effects were nullified by its extremes. Though generally orthodox, its emphasis on such spiritual gifts as continuance of prophetic revelation caused it to be condemned. The Church declared that Biblical revelation had come to an end and that special spiritual gifts were no longer operative.

During the third century three movements arose to challenge the authority and doctrinal solidarity of the Church: Novatianism, Monarchianism, and Manicheism. Novatian was Bishop of Rome 251–3 and was an able defender of the doctrine of the Trinity against the Monarchians. But he fell out with the hierarchy over the treatment of those who renounced their faith in the face of persecution and later sought renewal of fellowship with the Church. He denied the right of the Church to restore the lapsed and advocated a purist concept of Church membership that smacked of Montanistic legalism. The dissenting party chose him as bishop and the result was a schism that spread over most of the empire and lasted until the sixth century. Toward the end of the fourth century the hierarchy began to treat Novatianists as heretics.

Monarchianism was more strictly a doctrinal error. The problem the Monarchians faced was maintenance of the unity of the Godhead in the face of Trinitarianism. Their solution was something less than orthodox. Some of them, like the later Socinians and Unitarians, taught that the Father alone possessed true personality; the Logos and Holy Spirit were merely impersonal attributes of the Godhead. So the power of God came upon the man Jesus and gradually penetrated and deified His humanity. But Jesus was not to be considered God in the truest sense of the word. Other Monarchians viewed the three persons of the Godhead as merely modes of expression or ways of describing God. They were not distinct divine persons. This modalistic type of Monarchianism also came to be known as Sabellianism and Noetianism after two of its leading exponents. The Monarchians called forth extensive and effective definition of the Trinitarian position. But while Monarchianism was dealt fatal body blows by the Polemicists, there have repeatedly arisen in Christendom groups holding the Unitarian position.

Manicheism has been described as Gnosticism with its Christian elements reduced to a minimum and oriental elements raised to a maximum. The system was developed by Mani in Southern Babylonia about 240 and thereafter rapidly spread through Persia, India, China, Egypt, North Africa and Italy. It became the official religion of Turkey. Its appeal was great, even claiming such leaders as St. Augustine among its adherents for a time. After a somewhat meteoric initial success, Manicheism rapidly lost ground and died out—probably in part because of the sterile rigidity which the system early attained.

Like Gnosticism, Manicheism was a dualistic system. The kingdom of darkness at one time attacked the kingdom of light and the result was a mixed creation of light and darkness (good and evil) in which the kingdom of light is engaged in a program of gradual purification. Christ came into the world to aid the good principle in man to overcome the thrusts of the kingdom of darkness.

At the moment we are less concerned with the teachings of Mani than its effects. In their system there were two classes: the elect and the auditors. The former alone were admitted to the secret rites of baptism and communion, which were celebrated with great pomp. The elect were very ascetic and occupied themselves with religious exercises. The auditors participated in the holiness of the elect in return for supplying the elect with the necessities of life. Manicheism helped to foster the ascetic spirit in the churches and was in large measure responsible for the division of church members into clergy and laity. Moreover, it promoted the growth of the priestly function or the belief that ministers are intermediaries between God and man and have extraordinary power with God.

The effects of the perversions in the early Church were both negative and positive. They introduced erroneous views and practices into the regular churches and hindered their growth and development. On the other hand, they forced Church leaders to formulate more clearly the doctrines of the Church and to establish the limits of the canon which could furnish a source of truth for combating error.

Chapter IV

ESTABLISHMENT OF CANON AND CREED

Books for a New Testament

SOME SEEM TO HAVE THE ATTITUDE that the books to be included in the New Testament canon were decided on hastily, by a group of early Church leaders, late on a hot summer afternoon. And perhaps the choice of those men was no better than a comparable group of Church officials would make in the twentieth century. The facts of history demonstrate, however, that the New Testament was not formed hastily, nor was it formed by the councils. It was the product of centuries of development, and its official ratification came in response to the practical needs of the churches.

Several developments forced the Church to formulate a canon of the New Testament. First, by the end of the first century contemporary witnesses to the message of Jesus and the Apostles were mostly gone. The oral traditions became corrupt and conflicting, and believers wanted a body of Scripture which would spell out the authoritative message of the Apostles. Second, from the beginning of the Church it was customary to read Scripture in the worship services for edification of believers.[1] Increasingly church leaders became concerned that the readings be truly the message of God for the people. Third, such

---

[1] At first such readings were taken from the Old Testament only. Later they were chosen from the "Memoirs of the Apostles." The fact that Judaism had formed an Old Testament canon was important for establishing the principle of canonicity which would lead eventually to a New Testament canon.

heretics as Marcion [2] were formulating canons to promote their own special viewpoint. Marcion about A.D. 140 composed a canon of a mutilated Luke and ten of Paul's Epistles. He rejected the Old Testament. In self defense the Church had to decide what books belonged in the canon.

Fourth, about the same time that Marcion and the Gnostics were making great inroads into the established churches, the Montanists began to promulgate ideas of continuing revelation. As noted in the last chapter, the Church in retaliation declared that Biblical revelation had ceased. Fifth, a large number of obviously apocryphal works began to appear in increasing numbers. These gospels, acts, and epistles attempted to fill in gaps in the narrative of the life of Christ and the Apostles and to round out the theological message of the Church. Some of these books were obviously not on a par with the books we now recognize as canonical but others were very close to the New Testament message. An effort needed to be made to separate the wheat from the chaff. Last, the persecutions called for a decision on the contents of the New Testament canon. For instance, the Diocletian persecution in 303 called for the burning of all sacred books and the punishment of those who possessed them. Preservation of Scripture in the face of such determined imperial opposition required great effort and endangered the lives of those who hid or copied it. Therefore one wanted to be sure he was expending effort or risking his life to disseminate or protect a genuine work.

We have been talking about the need for forming a canon, but have not yet defined what we mean by the term. It came from the Greek word which meant *measuring*

---

[2] Marcion, a native of Asia Minor who went to Rome, is sometimes classified as a Gnostic. While his teachings bear resemblance to those of the Gnostics, he differed from them greatly at many points.

rod and came to signify that which serves as a measure or standard or that which meets a certain standard. In the second century the term was applied to the Rule of Faith—an early form of the Apostles' Creed—which was employed as a measure or test of one's orthodoxy. In the third and fourth centuries it was applied to New Testament Scripture. Canonical Scripture, then, is that which on the one hand provides a standard of doctrine and holy living and which, on the other hand, meets the standard or tests of inspiration.

It is one thing to determine the need for a canon; it is quite another to decide what belongs in it. Tests of canonicity had to be employed. Early it was suggested by Church Fathers that those books were canonical which were inspired. But inspiration is rather intangible and subject to differences of opinion. So secondary tests were used. One of the most important of these was apostolicity: that is, was a book written by an Apostle or someone very close to the Apostles. Thus, Luke's Gospel was accepted because of his close relationship with Paul; Mark's because of his close association with Peter and Paul. Of course Matthew and John were Apostles. Then there was the test of internal appeal. Did a book contain moral or doctrinal elements inferior to the standards set by the Apostles in their acknowledged writings?

As these and other tests were applied in various ways over the centuries, the canon gradually developed. Conservatives have long held that all of the New Testament books were written by about the end of the first century, in spite of liberal claims to the contrary. And archaeological evidence now quite effectively confirms the conservative position. It seems that almost from the time of their composition the four Gospels and Acts were accepted as divinely inspired accounts of the life of Christ and the development of the early Church. As Paul addressed his epistles to various churches, they accepted his word to them as coming from the mouth of God. And gradually nearby churches came to feel that letters sent to sister churches were of value for them too; so they made copies. In this way the Pauline Epistles began to circulate individually and by the end of the second century as a collection. The story concerning the rest of the New Testament books is not so simple.

Testimony in the writings of the Church Fathers to the existence and value of various New Testament books is extensive—beginning as early as the end of the first century with Clement of Rome. And there are other notable pieces of evidence. A full catalog of this information is quite out of the question; a few of the outstanding items are noted here. About the middle of the second century Tatian composed the first harmony of the Gospels. A decade or two later a canon was drawn up, now bearing the name Muratori after the Italian archaeologist who published it. The work is not quite complete in the condition it has come to us. It recognizes the four Gospels, Acts, the Pauline Epistles, Revelation, two (or three) epistles of John, and Jude. And it adds the Apocalypse of Peter and omits I and II Peter and Hebrews and possibly one of John's epistles.

From the time of Irenaeus (c. 175) the canon was thought to contain essentially the same books we have in it today, though there were continuing disputes over some inclusions. Clement of Alexandria (c. 200) seemed to recognize all of the New Testament books. The great Origen (c. 250) divided the books into categories of universally accepted and disputed works. In the former he put four Gospels, thirteen epistles of Paul, I Peter, I John, Acts, and Revelation. In the latter he put Hebrews, II Peter, II and III John, James, Jude and four works not now included in the New Testament. He himself seems to have accepted nearly all New Testament books. Hebrews was disputed because the authorship was uncertain; II Peter because it differed in style and vocabulary from I Peter; James and Jude because they represented themselves as servants rather than apostles of Christ; in II and III John the author called himself an elder rather than an apostle. Eusebius, the great historian of the fourth century, also divided New Testament books into various categories. In the group of disputed books he included the same ones as had Origen. By the time of the Council of Carthage in 397 only the twenty-seven books we now accept were adopted as canonical. The same decision was rendered at Carthage in 419. But those were local councils; their decision was ratified at the Ecumenical Council of Chalcedon in 451. Since that time there has been no continuing conflict on the subject.

Thus it can readily be seen that the story of the formation of the New Testament canon was a long one—not involving any hasty decision on the part of an ecclesiastical body. Basically, three steps were involved in the process: divine inspiration, gradual human recognition and acceptance of the separate works, and official ratification or adoption of those books already universally accepted in the Church.

CONTROVERSIES AND CREEDS

Just as the New Testament Canon developed in response to a need in the Church, so did the creeds. In the days before the canon was formulated and when there were few copies of any of the New Testament books in circulation, believers required some standard to keep them in the path of orthodoxy. Moreover, they needed a standard by which to test heretical opinions. So very early, possibly near the end of the first century or beginning of the second, a rule of faith came into existence.

Assuming different forms in different churches, it generally taught that Christ, the Son of God, suffered under Pontius Pilate, was crucified and died, was buried, rose again, and ascended into Heaven—for the remission of sins. This rule of faith, which has come to be called the Apostles' Creed, reached its present form about 750.

Other creeds were formulated too—in an effort to settle controversies which tore the Church into opposing factions. Some of the controversies had to do with the nature of Christ, some with the Holy Spirit, and one with the nature of man. These doctrinal quarrels were handled very differently from those of the second and third centuries. When Christianity became a legal religion early in the fourth century, the Emperor Constantine regarded himself as head of the Christian religion along with the other religions of state. Therefore, when difficulties arose he called a Church-wide or ecumenical council to deal with the matter and to formulate a statement (creed) of settlement. Other emperors followed the same practice. While these struggles concerning Christ, the Holy Spirit, and man were going on concurrently, for the sake of clearer presentation they are separated here.

A. *Controversies Concerning the Nature of Christ.* About 318, Arius, an elder of Alexandria, found great difficulty in accepting the trinitarian nature of the Godhead and began to teach that Christ was different in essence from the Father—that there was a time when He did not exist and that He was created by the Father. Athanasius, arch-deacon of Alexandria, rose to meet the challenge, asserting that Christ and the Father were the same in essence and that the Son was eternal. His primary concern was that if Christ were a mere creature, faith in Him could not bring salvation to man. The controversy raged. The fact that a synod at Alexandria deposed Arius in 321 did not end the struggle. Arius was able to win over some of the leading churchmen of the East, and matters only grew worse. Finally Constantine felt obliged to step in and restore harmony. He called an ecumenical council at Nicea, in northwest Asia Minor. Over 300 bishops, in addition to a number of lesser dignitaries, attended. Ultimately the majority and the Emperor himself were persuaded to throw their weight behind Athanasius, and a creed was drawn up in 325 which declared that the Son was the same in essence with the Father, the only begotten of the Father, and very God of very God. But the troubles of the Athanasian party had only begun. In the see-sawing fortunes of subsequent years, Athanasius was banished by the Emperor no less than five times, with the consequent restoration of Arius. Gradually, however, the situation changed and the orthodox party enjoyed a definite majority in the empire.

In the process of asserting the full deity of Christ, some theologians had done so at the expense of His humanity. They taught that a complete humanity could not be sinless and that the divine nature while assuming a human body, took the place of the higher rational principle in man. Several synodical meetings condemned the idea of the defective humanity of Christ, and finally the ecumenical council of Constantinople in 381 asserted His true and full humanity.

Then a third issue arose. If Christ was both fully divine and human, how were the two natures related in one person. Nestorius, Bishop of Constantinople, was one of those who saw the two natures in loose mechanical conjunction. Neither nature shared in the properties of the other; so the divine did not have a part in the sufferings of the human nature of Christ. It will be readily seen that this is not merely an academic question. As Cyril of Alexandria pointed out, if Nestorius were right, a sinner would be redeemed by the sufferings of a mere man, and a mere man could accomplish no redemption. The Nestorian controversy led to the calling of a third ecumenical council at Ephesus in 431. The council met and anathematized the teachings of Nestorius before the Nestorian party arrived. When the outlawed party arrived, it set up a rival council. The Emperor finally decided against the Nestorians and Nestorius entered a monastery. The result of the council was to demonstrate that the majority of bishops were in favor of the doctrines of Cyril (who argued for a true union of the two natures), but clarification of the matter was left to a later council.

Following the Council of Ephesus there was a great deal of dissatisfaction on the part of many. As has just been pointed out, the Council of Ephesus was not a true meeting of minds in an effort to resolve issues. Moreover, Eutyches, abbot of a monastery near Constantinople, in an effort to demonstrate the true unity of the person of Christ, began to teach that after the incarnation of Christ the two natures fused into one so that the one nature partook of the properties of the other. Distinctions between the two natures were obliterated. His arguments heightened the controversy considerably. Again it should be pointed out that we are not dealing here with mere academic issues. Complete confusion reigns if Eutyches was right. Omniscience is an attribute of Deity only; according to the flesh Christ grew in wisdom and knowledge and favor with God and men. Omnipresence is an attribute of Deity only; one of the important characteristics of a human body is that it is confined to a specific locality. If Christ is already physically omnipresent, how can He come a second time from Heaven? At length a new general council was called at Chalcedon in 451. Its decision was that Christ was truly God, truly man, that the two natures were united in one person without confusion, change, division or separation.

Like the other councils discussed above, the Council of Chalcedon did not bring final settlement. In Palestine, Egypt, and Syria groups arose to perpetuate the teachings of Cyril and Eutyches. They held out strongly for one nature in Christ. Ultimately they were able to force a fifth ecumenical council, the second at Constantinople, in 553, which ratified the Chalcedonian creed but made changes which tended to favor the Eutychians.

After the Second Constantinopolitan Council, another conflict arose over the Person of Christ—to the effect that there was only one will in Christ. Otherwise, they held, Christ would have sinned because certainly the human will would have succumbed to temptation. Ultimately a council, the third at Constantinople, in 680–81, met to deal with this issue. The decision was to ratify the Chalcedonian Creed with the addition that Christ had two wills, the human and divine, the human will being subject to the divine.

While these great ecumenical councils did not settle for all time discussion concerning the nature of the person of Christ, they did set forth the chief elements which have characterized an orthodox Christology down through the ages: His true and full deity, His true and full humanity, the true union of the two natures in one person, without fusion or confusion.

B. *Controversies Concerning the Holy Spirit.* Reference has already been made to Montanist and Monarchian perversions of the doctrine of the Holy Spirit. And in connection with the Council of Nicea something has been said about Arius. A further word needs to be said here, however. Not only did Arius hold that Christ was different in essence from the Father, he also taught that the Holy Spirit was different in essence. In fact, he seems to have believed that the Holy Spirit was the creature of a creature, i. e., of Christ. Being particularly concerned with Christological problems, the Nicene Council did not make detailed pronouncement concerning the Holy Spirit. It merely affirmed, "I believe in one Holy Spirit." But after the Nicene Council, further attacks of the Arian sort (known as Macedonianism because espoused by Macedonius) on the deity of the Holy Spirit brought forth an array of orthodox literature. The result was that at the First Council of Constantinople in 381 phrases were included in the creed which asserted that the Holy Spirit was to be worshiped and glorified as was the Father, that He proceeded from the Father, and that He was responsible for revelation. In succeeding decades the doctrine of His deity was further defined, and the Council of Chalcedon in 451 made the declarations of the First Council of Constantinople more explicit.

C. *Controversy Concerning Man.* The controversy concerning the nature of man was the only one that took place in the Western part of the Empire; all the rest took place in the East. Chief protagonists in the struggle were St. Augustine, Bishop of Hippo in North Africa, and Pelagius, a British monk who ultimately found his way to North Africa. These men formed their views independently of each other, not in reaction to one another. Soon after arriving at Carthage, Pelagius clashed head on with the prevailing theological viewpoint; and the controversy spread rapidly to other provinces. Pelagius taught that Adam's sin affected only himself; man is still born on the same plane as Adam. There was, therefore, no such thing as original sin. Sin involved an act of the will and was due to the bad example of Adam and society since Adam's time. Man's salvation is possible without law or gospel; some attained salvation before the period of the law, and of course the gospel came after that.

Augustine, on the other hand, held to the unity of the race, that all had sinned in Adam. So men sin because they are sinners and are totally depraved—unable to do good unto salvation. God therefore had to exercise grace in order to achieve the salvation of man. Some He elected unto salvation and some He predestined to reprobation. Salvation was for him a work of God from start to finish.

Pelagius experienced considerable opposition almost as soon as he arrived in North Africa. He was condemned by a Carthaginian Synod in 412, by Pope Innocent I in 416, by a general council of African churches in 418, and finally by the ecumenical council at Ephesus in 431.

But this did not mean the triumph of Augustinianism. Augustine was out of step with the Church of his day. He stressed too much the inner Christian life and too little the external ceremonies; he denied the eucharist had any sin-atoning power apart from the faith of the partaker; while advocating asceticism, he denied it had any value apart from transformation of life into Christlikeness. He opposed the predominant sacramental nature of achieving salvation in his time. So while Pelagianism was condemned, a sort of semi-Pelagianism was to win out in the Church—a system in which grace and human works were to join together in achieving salvation within the framework of the Church and the sacramental system.

The years during which the first six great ecumenical councils met (325–681) were turbulent ones. They were years during which the Church was torn asunder by theological controversy—controversy which produced great statements of faith. They were also years when the barbarians were chipping away at the borders of the Roman Empire, conquering the whole western portion of it. And they were years when the hierarchal Church was developing its doctrine and organizational machinery. Let us now take a quick look at the rise and decline of the Roman Church during the Middle Ages.

Chapter V

THE MEDIEVAL PAPACY

BEGINNINGS

THE ROMAN CATHOLIC and Eastern Orthodox Churches as they existed at the end of the Middle Ages and as they appear in the twentieth century are a product of historical evolution. While apologists for the Roman Catholic Confession have been particularly adept at finding precedents for new dogmas and organizational developments they have propounded, an objective view of history has not always been so convincing.

In the New Testament the office of bishop is placed alongside that of elder and deacon—whether equatable with either of those offices it is not our purpose now to discuss. With Ignatius (about 110) arose the view that elders were to obey the bishop, and the congregation was to obey both. In other words, he taught the supremacy of of a bishop in a local church. By the end of the second century, Irenaeus was asserting the unity of the Church (a spiritual unity, not organic) by virtue of its headship in Christ and community of belief as handed down through a succession of elders. Thereafter a tendency arose to transform the spiritual unity into an organic unity. By the middle of the third century the influential Cyprian, Bishop of Carthage, taught that the Universal Church (outside of which there was no salvation) was ruled over by bishops who were the successors of the Apostles. Apostolic authority, he held, was first given to Peter. So the Church at Rome became predominant because he was believed to have founded it. Moreover, Cyprian asserted the priestly function of the clergy.

The views of these men were widely received in the Church. So, by the time Christianity became a tolerated religion during Constantine's day, the concepts of the priestly function of the clergy, apostolic succession, the ruling bishop, and the recognition of the Roman bishop as first among equals were established. Now it remained for the Roman bishop to transform his primacy into supremacy.

Rome's competition came particularly from Constantinople, Antioch, Jerusalem, Ephesus, and Alexandria.[1] Soon, however, Jerusalem ceased to present a problem because the Romans destroyed the city in 135; Ephesus lost out because the area was torn by the Montanist schism during the second century.

There were several reasons why Rome could effectively compete against the others in her struggle for supremacy. First of all, she claimed Petrine foundation. Peter was chief of the Apostles and the one, according to Rome, on whom the Church was founded. And the dogma of apostolic succession, while recognizing that other bishops could trace their authority to other Apostles, would grant prominence to Peter's successors. Second, the Bishop of Rome was superior in the West, while bishops of Constantinople, Antioch, and Alexandria competed for supremacy within a relatively small area in the East.

---

[1] Bishops arose all over the Empire, largely in response to administrative needs of the churches and as leaders in the war against heresy. Because of their location, certain bishops achieved special prominence. In 325, at the Council of Nicea the bishops of Alexandria, Antioch, and Rome were given authority over divisions of the Empire in which they were located. By the fifth century Rome was asserting that her primacy was intended in the arrangement.

Third, after the move of the capital from Rome to Constantinople in 330, political power in the West gradually declined. With the barbarian invasion and the chaos that ensued, the Bishop of Rome became the most powerful figure there. He represented the only alive institution; and the Church took on civil functions. In Constantinople, on the other hand, the continuing Roman Empire maintained itself through varying fortunes until 1453. There the bishop found himself subservient to the emperor and therefore less capable of asserting himself. In this connection, it should be pointed out that when the power of the imperial government was weak, it was sometimes advantageous to the emperor to recognize the pretensions of Rome, in which case the Bishop of Rome held virtual authority over the Bishop of Constantinople. Finally, the Church in the West was not constantly rent asunder by doctrinal controversy as was the Church in the East. And in the midst of the controversies that did arise, the Church at Rome always proved to be orthodox. So Rome was in a much stronger position to develop her program and extend her influence than were churches of the East.

In discussing the period of the beginnings of the Roman Church (prior to the pivotal pontificate of Gregory I in 590), several important persons and developments should be mentioned. The formation of the canon and creeds has already been described, as has been the rise of errors and their effect on the development of Roman Catholic doctrine and practice. We have also noted the contributions of the Church Fathers, especially those of Augustine the great theologian and Jerome the translator of the Vulgate. But a few others require comment at this point. The first of these is Leo I (440–461). He did much to advance the cause of the papacy. Taking advantage of disorder resulting from the Vandal conquest of the province of Africa, he managed to secure the recognition of his author-

ity by the Catholic Church there. He interfered in the
affairs of the Church in Gaul to the advantage of papal
power, and he asserted his authority in Illyricum (Yugo-
slavia). By means of his statesmanship, he saved Rome
from being sacked by the Huns and the Vandals; in the
process he added much to his prestige. And he obtained
from the Emperor Valentinian III the declaration that
bishops everywhere were to be subservient to the pope at
Rome and that governors of provinces were to compel
bishops to go to Rome when summoned by the pope.

Gelasius (492-496) instituted the claim of moral superintendence over political rulers on the part of the pope.
While there were two spheres of rule, the spiritual and
temporal, he claimed that the Church must give account
to God for the deeds of kings, and so the king must
submit to the Church in spiritual matters. Symmachus
(498–514) added the dictum that no tribunal could compel the appearance of a pope or sentence him in his
absence.

But of particular importance was the conversion of
Clovis, a Frankish chieftain, in 496. Soon afterward three
thousand of his followers were baptized into the Roman
Church. For Clovis this move was vital because it won
for him the support of the Catholics in the West, where
he was the only orthodox Catholic prince. Ultimately he
was able to conquer Gaul, Burgundy and Bavaria. The
Church also profited from his conversion because he
zealously supported it and gave considerable land to it.
In other words, the relation of Clovis and the Roman
Church was mutually beneficial—each leaning on the
other for help. As we shall see later on, this relationship
ultimately led to the full alliance of Church and State in
the Holy Roman Empire of Charlemagne.

GREGORY AND HIS SUCCESSORS

Gregory I, the Great (540–604), was one of the greatest leaders that the Roman Church has ever had. Coming on the scene at a time of widespread political confusion with its consequent effects on the life and organization of the Church, he became a stabilizing influence politically and was largely responsible for the creation of the medieval papacy. Sprung from a noble, wealthy and devout family, Gregory early turned to the monastic life as a way to glorify God. And he spent his inherited fortune to found seven monasteries. For several years he represented the Roman bishop at Constantinople and in 590 was elected bishop of Rome.

Gregory never called himself pope, but he exercised all the power of later popes—maintaining more or less effective control over the churches of the western part of the Empire. And he would not let anyone else among his contemporaries lay claim to a Church-wide authority. One of Gregory's great struggles was with John, the Patriarch of Constantinople, who claimed to be universal bishop. Gregory opposed John but did not assert his own power in retaliation; he merely claimed to be the "servant of the servants of the Lord."

For many reasons, Gregory was one of the most important popes in the history of Romanism. As noted above, he transformed the bishopric of Rome into a papal system that endured through the Middle Ages. Secondly, he introduced changes into the liturgy and sought the standardization of it. While Gregory was not responsible for the type of chant which bears his name, he did much to promulgate the use of the chant in worship services. Third, from a theological standpoint, he served as something of a Grand Central Station of the early Church. The lines of thought found in the Councils and Fathers

meet in his system. Though not original, he is important
for his definition and discussion of several items that
were part of the popular piety of the day. In this regard,
his views on angelology, demonology, purgatory, the
Eucharist, and the efficacy of relics are particularly important. His theology is a sort of watered down Augustinianism combined with superstitious and mythological
views of his day.

Fourth, he was important for his writings. The
Moralia, a commentary on Job, provides one of the patterns for the allegorical interpretation of Scripture common during the Middle Ages. His superstitious nature
and that of the age is well displayed in his *Dialogues,*
which concerns the lives and miracles of pious fathers
in Italy. And his *Pastoral Rule* was a practical work which
instructed the bishop in the care of his flock. Gregory
was a good preacher too, as evidenced by his forty sermons that have survived. Gregory's writings have earned
for him a place among the four great Latin doctors of
the Western Church: Ambrose, Augustine, Jerome, Gregory. Fifth, Gregory promoted asceticism in the Church,
especially as he enforced the celibacy of the clergy and
as he restored monastic [2] discipline. Lastly, Gregory possessed great missionary zeal. He sent forty monks to
England in 597 under the leadership of Augustine (not
the famous Bishop of Hippo who died in 430). Their
success was pronounced, especially in the area of Can-

---

[2] Monasticism with its ascetic approach to life arose very early
in the East, where its adherents generally lived a hermit existence.
Basil of Caesarea developed the movement on more of a community or communal basis during the fourth century, and about
the same time the great Athanasius introduced it to the West.
But it was St. Benedict (c. 500) who was responsible for the general monastic rule of poverty, chastity, and obedience and the
type of monasticism which grew up in Western Europe—a type
that was more productive and practical than that of the East.

terbury, which became the religious capital of England and the seat of an archbishop.

For about a century Gregory's successors hardly maintained the high place he had earned for them. More than one of them was condemned as a heretic. And it was a period when Roman monks in Britain were engaged in a struggle for supremacy with Irish monks who preceded them there. For a long time missionary activity had been extensive in the British Isles. St. Patrick, a Scotchman, evangelized Ireland during the fifth century. Columba, an Irishman, returned the favor during the sixth century by becoming the Apostle to Scotland. Other Irish monks went north to the Shetlands, Hebrides, Orkneys and Iceland. And some moved southward into England. Meanwhile Columban and other Irish monks worked in Germany, Switzerland, and even Italy. The Irish monks differed at many points from the emissaries of the pope. St. Patrick, for instance, was closer to Protestantism in method and message than he was to his contemporaries. A contest was inevitable. After a number of contacts between the Irish and Romanists, at the Synod of Whitby in Northumbria in 664 the Romanists finally won out and the Irish monks withdrew northward. Already in 636 South Ireland submitted to the papacy and in 697 North Ireland followed suit.

Meanwhile, far to the East a new and much greater threat was rising to challenge the Medieval Church. In 622 Mohammed made his famous move from Mecca to Medina (Hegira) and thereafter began the successful period of his preaching. Constructing a theology which partook of elements of Judaism, Christianity, and Arabian heathenism, and infusing a fanatical zeal that brooked no opposition, he produced a steam roller movement that soon flattened the Middle East, North Africa, and part of Europe. In fact, Mohammedanism has gained adherents until it can claim about one-seventh of the world's population today.

While it is not the purpose of the present study to engage in theological discussion, Mohammedanism is so important in Western history that at least the five "pillars" which characterize the faithful should be noted: 1. Acceptance of the creed "There is no God but Allah and Mohammed is his prophet"; 2. Prayer five times a day toward Mecca; 3. Making a pilgrimage to Mecca at least once during a lifetime; 4. Giving alms for pious and charitable purposes; 5. Fasting from sunrise to sunset throughout the sacred month of Ramadan (corresponding to parts of our March and April). Often holy war is described as a sixth pillar.

Several factors contributed to the rapid spread of Mohammedanism. 1. A positive fanatical monotheistic program which promised positions of leadership and booty to those who would engage in world conquest was certainly a powerful incentive in obtaining followers. 2. The Roman Empire was rapidly decaying from within while it exhausted its resources and those of the Persian Empire as well in a gruelling fight almost to the death. Neither the Persians nor the Byzantines [3] were any match for the fanatical Arabs. 3. Moreover, the development of image worship in the Catholic Church made the Christianity of the day look polytheistic to both the Mohammedans and many Catholics. Therefore Mohammedanism with its monotheistic emphasis seemed to be superior.

Before his death in 632 Mohammed had won many followers in Arabia. His successor Abu Bakr (632–34) rapidly conquered the peninsula and at the same time sent volunteers into Syria and Persia. Omar (634–44) began systematic conquest of the Roman provinces. In

---

[3] Name applied to the Eastern Roman Empire, which became essentially Greek after the fall of the West to the barbarians.

635 he took Damascus. He completed conquest of Palestine in 640 and about the same time took most of the Persian Empire. Alexandria and most of Egypt surrendered in 642. Conquests continued rapidly under successive leaders. The Moslem fleet destroyed the Byzantine fleet in 655 and thereafter maintained naval control of the Mediterranean for five centuries. Between 685 and 705 the conquest of North Africa was completed, including the conversion of the Moors. In 711 the Mohammedans invaded Spain and in seven years reached the borders of France. On they went. It seemed as if all Europe were doomed. Meanwhile the advance continued into India.

At this point some abler popes came to the chair of St. Peter. And their efforts coincided with the continuing rise of the Frankish Kingdom and the efforts of great missionaries of the Church. The pontificate of Gregory II (715–731) was a time of especially great advance. Willibrord, a native of York in England succeeded in planting the standards of the Church among the wild peoples of Holland and Denmark. Meanwhile Boniface became the great missionary of Central Europe. With the support of Gregory II and Charles Martel, the real ruler of the Franks, he succeeded in reforming the Frankish churches, abolishing heathen customs, improving the morals of the priests, and systematizing church organization. Boniface brought the Frankish bishops to full support of Rome.

Back in Rome Gregory was having his troubles. Leo the Isaurian, Emperor at the time, sought to rid himself of the pope by violence because Gregory opposed Leo's taxation policies in Italy and his interference with the Church's use of images (to be discussed later). Supported by the people of Rome and the Lombards in Northern Italy, Gregory managed to die a natural death.

Contemporary with Gregory II lived one of England's best known sons, the Venerable Bede, a monk who worked at the monasteries of Jarrow and Wearmouth near Newcastle. While he wrote various Biblical works (about forty in number), they are overshadowed by his *Ecclesiastical History of the English People*. This book provides us with much important detail concerning early English Church history, and it earned for the author the title "Father of English history."

At the beginning of the rule of Gregory III (731–741) it looked as if Romanism were doomed in Western Europe. The Lombards got out of hand and threatened to destroy the Church in Italy. But the greater danger was posed by the Mohammedans advancing steadily north into France. Charles Martel, not actual king of the Franks but mayor of the palace, summoned enough force to turn back the Mohammedan hordes at Tours in central France in 732. This was one of the most important events in the history of the West. A defeat for Charles on this occasion would have resulted in the predominance of Oriental culture and Mohammedanism in Europe. Charles Martel also came to the aid of the pope in his struggle with the Lombards. Negotiations began during these years for an alliance between the Franks and the papacy. And the next half century was characterized by increasing relations between the king and the pope, the king often coming to the aid of the pope. In fact, in 752 Boniface anointed Pepin, son of Charles Martel, king of the Franks—a foreshadowing of the time when the pope would anoint Charlemagne.

CHURCH-STATE ALLIANCE

The year 800 serves as a pivotal date in history. On Christmas day in Rome Leo III crowned Charlemagne the first emperor of the Holy Roman Empire. The empire was called Roman because it was to succeed the now defunct power of Rome in the West. It was called holy because it was to be supreme over Christendom. This new arrangement constituted a full alliance between the pope and emperor because each was to have world-wide dominion within his own sphere and each was to cooperate with the other and promote the interests of the other. Beyond the immediate significance, the concept of the Holy Roman Empire was to have some long-range effects on European history. For a thousand years one European ruler or another tore up the countryside with his armies in an effort to establish himself as successor of the Caesars. Finally in 1806 Napoleon abolished the empire.

Charlemagne was able to control the vast territory of France, Germany, Switzerland, and Italy. And in the process he maintained rather effective rule over the pope. His three sons were not so capable, and after their death the empire was dismembered. Thereafter the process of disintegration went rapidly forward until Europe was divided into a host of small antagonistic principalities.[4] And after the days of Charlemagne's son Lothair, the popes were able to be their own masters; lands around Rome that had been ruled by the emperor fell into the hands of the popes.

It is purposed to include under this heading of Church-State Alliance the whole period from 800 to 1073. The papacy reached a high point of development when allied with the Carlovingian house; but it declined with the fortunes of that house and the political disintegration of

---

[4] It is true that there was some success at restoration of the Holy Roman Empire, such as that accomplished in the days of Otto the Great about the middle of the tenth century; but none could re-establish the empire of Charlemagne. From the days of Otto we see a very definite Germanization of the empire. The emperor became nothing more than a German noble elected by his peers to be king of Germany.

Europe. We shall observe the papacy picking itself up by the boot straps in 1073 in an effort to usher in a new day of glory.

By the time of Pope John VIII (872–882) the Carlovingian Empire was definitely coming to an end. John, harrassed by local enemies and the Mohammedans, turned to the Carlovingian Charles the Bald of Germany for help—agreeing to bestow the imperial crown on Charles. But Charles died before rescuing John, and there was no further effective help coming from Charlemagne's successors. The Pope was forced to make a humiliating treaty with the Mohammedans and to agree to pay annual tribute to keep them out of Rome. During much of the period 880–1000, Italy was in anarchy, and the papacy suffered accordingly. For instance, there were twelve popes 882–903. The chair of St. Peter was occupied by some very unworthy individuals between about 880 and 1050. For example, near the end of the period Benedict IX was pope. Even such an impartial source as the *Encyclopaedia Britannica* notes that he became pope at twelve, was guilty of gross disorders of conduct, and was driven out of Rome by the local population on more than one occasion because of his disorderly conduct. But it is not our purpose to portray the papacy at its worst. As a matter of fact, one is amazed that the popes were as capable as they were and that they could advance the cause of the papacy under such great handicaps.

Surprisingly enough, the papacy extended its territory greatly between 800 and 1073. About the middle of the ninth century an archbishopric was established at Hamburg. Christianity entered Norway via England in the tenth century. About 1000 Norwegian missionaries won Iceland to Christianity, and shortly thereafter Lief the Lucky evangelized Greenland. About the same time Bohemia, Hungary, and Poland became Roman Catholic nations. Meanwhile the Eastern Church was evangelizing to the North. Cyril and Methodius were very successful in Bulgaria during the ninth century. During the tenth and eleventh centuries Russia was won over. By means of the baptism of King Vladimir in 988, the Eastern Slavs were turned in a body to Christianity—just as the Franks had been by the baptism of Clovis.

Not only did the Church greatly extend her territory during the period 800–1073, she also greatly extended her power. With the fragmentizing of Europe politically, the pope often stood a better chance of bringing princes, particularly the lesser ones, to terms. As Christianity spread and with it the idea that salvation came only through membership in the true Church, the threat of excommunication was often enough to bring rulers to terms. If it was not, the papacy would try interdict—withholding services of the Church from the people of a whole area. Usually the populace brought enough pressure on the king or noble to insure a victory for the pope.

One more development needs to be considered before going on to view the medieval papacy at its height: the split between the Eastern Orthodox and Roman Catholic branches of the Church. Several factors were responsible for the split. The first of these was the iconoclastic controversy or the controversy over the use of images. Leo the Isaurian in 726 had issued the first decree against their use—in large measure to meet the Mohammedan charge that Christianity was polytheistic. He was supported by the Patriarch of Constantinople and the higher clergy, but he was opposed by many of the monks and the common people. Gregory II at Rome denounced imperial interference—partly because the problem hardly existed in the West and partly because Rome held that political power had no right to interfere in the affairs of the Church. The controversy produced a definite breach between Rome and Constantinople. Gregory III was the last pope to seek confirmation of his election from Constantinople, and in 781 the popes ceased mentioning the name of the emperor in dating their documents. It was not until 787 that a Church council in the East finally settled the matter in favor of the use of images, but by that time the damage to unity of the Church was done.

The conflict over the procession of the Holy Spirit, known as the Filioque Controversy was also instrumental in separating the two bodies. Third, there was an unwillingness on the part of the patriarch of Constantinople and the pope at Rome to be subservient to each other. Fourth, there was no sharp definition of the boundaries of the territories to be ruled by Rome and Constantinople, and frequent struggles arose over administration of border areas. Fifth, there were basic differences in cultural background and influence between East and West—differences which hindered understanding and cooperation. Sixth, the East was subservient to the emperor while the West insisted on independence from the state and the right of moral superintendence of rulers of state. Finally, in 1054 a Roman delegation laid the bull of excommunication on the altar of St. Sophia in Constantinople. Of course the Greek patriarch retaliated. Thus the schism was complete.

The Medieval Papacy at Its Height

A new chapter in papal history began in 1073 when Hildebrand assumed the chair of St. Peter under the name of Gregory VII. His program and philosophy were basic to the achievement of supremacy in Christendom attained by the popes of the thirteenth century. For some twenty years before he became pope, Hildebrand was the power behind the papal throne. During that time he succeeded in reforming papal election procedure. Formerly popes were elected by the people of Rome, often under the influence of the aristocracy. In Hildebrand's day the change was made to election by the college of cardinals, a procedure which is still in effect.

Gregory as pontiff held to the supremacy of the pope within the Church and over temporal rulers. He carried on an unrelenting program to reduce all bishops, abbots, and clergy to absolute subjection to the papacy and was quite successful. He saw three particular abuses which needed correcting: the marriage of the clergy, simony, and investiture by secular princes. Gregory issued a ban on clerical marriage in 1074 and thereby prevented the clergy from becoming a hereditary caste; instead they were to become loyal to the pope. On simony (the buying and selling of church offices) he made unrelenting warfare. The problem of lay investiture was another story.

For centuries the political leaders of Europe had been accustomed to appointing and investing with symbols of office the church leaders within their realm. This was understandable because under the feudal system the common people were tied to the soil in a hand-to-mouth existence. They did not have the income to support the Church. Therefore it was up to the rulers to do so. Their reasoning was that if they supported the Church they should rule it. Certainly they should have the right to choose the clergy whose salaries they were paying. The Church thought otherwise, insisting on the right to rule her own household.

The great test of strength during Gregory's pontificate arose over the choice of the archbishop of Milan. Gregory's opponent was Henry IV, emperor of the Holy Roman Empire; each had a candidate for office. Henry was at a disadvantage because he was also engaged in an internal power struggle with some of the Saxon nobles.

Gregory threatened excommunication if Henry IV did not comply; Henry answered with a council at Worms which rejected papal authority. Henry was excommunicated and an anathema pronounced against his subjects. The Saxon nobles then demanded that the anathema be lifted within a year or forfeit his throne. So ultimately Henry was forced to make his peace with Gregory. But in the ensuing years Henry won the last round; he marched on Rome, set up a pope of his own choice, and Gregory died in exile.

The papacy ultimately won the investiture struggle, however. At a concordat of Worms in 1122 the emperor consented to permit the Church to elect bishops and abbots and invest them with spiritual power. While elections were to be held in the presence of the king, he could not use simony or violence. Elected officials of the Church were to pledge allegiance to the temporal power.

Of great importance to the papacy in arriving at the zenith of her power were the Crusades. By this means she could direct the energies of Europe in a way that would bring her great advantage. While it is true that some went on the Crusades for economic reasons or adventure or other lesser reasons, the primary motive of the Crusades was religious. Crusades against the Moors in Spain and Moslems in Sicily had been launched long before the movement which we generally call the Crusades.

The event which sparked the Crusades was the conquest of Palestine by the Seljuk Turks during the eleventh century. These Mohammedans were much less kindly disposed toward pilgrims than other Mohammedans who had controlled Jerusalem since the seventh century. Gregory VII had hoped to organize a crusade before he died, but troubles with Henry prevented that. Finally, in response to an appeal by the Emperor Alexius I of the Eastern Empire, Pope Urban II inaugurated the Crusading movement at the Council of Clermont in 1095. A great host gathered from France, the Lowlands, and Italy and finally took Jerusalem in 1099. The Crusaders then set up the Kingdom of Jerusalem. The Second Crusade was preached by the famous Bernard of Clairvaux in 1147 in order to meet the Moslem threat to the northern borders of the Kingdom of Jerusalem. The king of France and the emperor of the Holy Roman Empire led the Crusade, but it was completely unsuccessful, leaving Jerusalem in greater danger than before. The crusading movement ground to a standstill until 1187 when Jerusalem was captured by Saladin and all Christendom was again aroused.

The Third Crusade (1189–92) is known as the Crusade of the Three Kings: Richard of England, Philip Augustus of France, and Frederick I of Germany. Frederick drowned on the way to Palestine; Philip stayed in Palestine for a very short time, leaving Richard to carry on the struggle alone. While he was unsuccessful in taking Jerusalem, he did win permission for pilgrims to enter Jerusalem. The Fourth Crusade began in 1201, under the leadership of Pope Innocent III. He urged the capture of Egypt as a base of operations against Palestine. When the army gathered, it found itself without shipping, which Venice agreed to supply—suggesting that the Crusaders take Constantinople to pay for provisions and transportation. This they did, with the result that Innocent gained control of both the Eastern Orthodox Church and the Eastern Empire, until 1261 when the Eastern Empire regained her independence. The last Crusade of any significance was conducted by Frederick II of Germany in 1229. By diplomacy he acquired Jerusalem, Bethlehem, Nazareth, and a corridor to the sea. But of course his success was short lived.

The Crusades ended in failure, with Jerusalem remaining in Moslem hands until 1917 when General Allenby captured the Holy City from the Turks. Yet it must be said that while the Crusades lasted the Church enjoyed wave after wave of popular enthusiasm in support of her causes. Moreover, while the Church directed the energies of Europeans in fighting an external foe, she provided a safety valve which spared her a great deal of internal stress.

Directing the affairs of the medieval papacy at the very height of her power was Innocent III (1198-1216). As has already been noted, he controlled the Eastern Church and Empire. He humiliated Philip Augustus of France, forcing him to take back his divorced wife who appealed to the Pope. This Innocent did by laying an interdict on the whole nation of France. Shortly thereafter he humbled King John of England in a struggle over the appointment of a new archbishop of Canterbury. Again Innocent used the method of interdict, as well as inviting Philip of France to invade England if John refused to come to terms. About the same time Innocent interfered in the affairs of Germany, dictating the imperial succession there. Again he used a threat of French troops to accomplish his aim. Lastly, Innocent called the Fourth Lateran Council in 1215 to settle certain doctrinal matters. It decided that annual confession to a priest was mandatory for all laymen. And it enunciated the dogma of transubstantiation, which means that the bread and wine become the actual body and blood of Christ upon pronouncement of the priest. The priest could then perform an actual sacrifice of Christ every time the mass is said.

One of the strengths of the medieval papacy in maintaining her power over the populace of Western Europe was the Inquisition. Instituted by Gregory IX (1227-41), it was designed to inquire into the spread of heresy and to call before its tribunals Catholics suspected of heresy with a view to securing their repentance. The program was launched merely to keep the faithful in line, not to obtain the conversion of Jews and Moslems. The great purges against those peoples in Spain were inventions of the Spanish throne. The Inquisition became a necessity because of the spread of groups such as the Waldenses (discussed in Chapter VI), which threatened the very life of the papacy if allowed to go unchecked. The secular arm undertook to administer trial, torture, and killing of unrepentant persons. The Church has not, therefore, been willing to take the blame for the excesses which history records.

It has already been noted that at the height of her power the medieval papacy defined the dogma of transubstantiation and declared the necessity of annual confession to a priest. Other dogmas and doctrines were being formulated at this time too—largely through the efforts of the Scholastics. Scholasticism is hard to define adequately, but certain generalizations may be made concerning it. It was the sum of the teachings and methods of the prominent Western philosophers most widely accepted during the Middle Ages. It constituted a harmonization of philosophy and theology in one system for the purpose of rational demonstration of theological truth. The Scholastics sought certainty of the truth and salvation by way of knowledge and reason. The ninth to the twelfth centuries mark the formative period of Scholasticism, the thirteenth century the height, and the fourteenth and fifteenth centuries a period of decline. Anselm and Abelard are usually thought of as co-founders; Hugo and Peter Lombard as important representatives along the way; Thomas Aquinas as representing the movement at its height, and Duns Scotus and William of Ockam as typical writers during the period of decline.

The Scholastics and especially Aquinas are responsible for bringing to final formulation the sacramental system of the Roman Church—a system through which one was to obtain salvation. By the time they came on the scene the number of sacraments had been pegged at seven. They went on to spell out in greater detail the significance of baptism, the eucharist, confirmation, penance, extreme unction, holy orders, and marriage. Also, they set forth theories of the atonement still common today, defined the way of salvation, and in general formulated the theology of the Roman Church as it was approved at the Council of Trent and as it is authoritatively held at the present time.

Contemporary with the Scholastic movement came mysticism, which aimed at a certainty of salvation and the truth through experience. Some of the mystics went to great excess in their emphasis on a love experience with God but many of them seem to have been genuine believers. Three of the better mystics—all of the twelfth century—were Richard and Hugh of St. Victor and Bernard of Clairvaux. The latter is well known for his famous hymn, "Jesus the Very Thought of Thee." Mysticism and Scholasticism were a good counterbalance for each other. Mysticism kept Scholasticism from being too academic, and Scholasticism helped the mystics keep their feet on the ground.

In a very real sense it may be said that the backbone of the medieval papacy was the monastic movement. Long is the roll of great leaders of the Middle Ages who came from the monastery. It includes such famous names as Gregory I and VII, Richard and Hugh of St. Victor, and Bernard of Clairvaux. The monasteries were the conservatories of learning, centers of missionary and philanthropic work. The monks were the writers, preachers, philosophers, and theologians of the age; they headed the Crusades and the Inquisition. And it may be said that the monasteries provided something of a safety valve for the Roman Church, for in them earnest Christians had a great deal more freedom from ecclesiastical machinery than they would have had outside the cloister. Without this freedom, it is possible that much of the evangelical life would have parted company with Romanism sooner than it did. It should be remembered that Luther, Erasmus, and many other critics of the papacy had monastic backgrounds.

St. Benedict (about 500) developed the Western European form of monastic life, and other orders were in general offshoots of the Benedictine order. The Cluniac order came into being in 910, the Cistercian in 1098. The latter's most illustrious son was Bernard of Clairvaux. St. Francis of Assisi founded the Franciscan order in 1210 and St. Dominic, the Dominicans in 1215. The Augustinian order was formed out of a number of older bodies in 1244. The thirteenth century was the heydey of monasticism. It declined at the end of the century and throughout the fourteenth. There was some reform in the fifteenth century. The Reformation destroyed most of the monasteries of Northern Europe and seriously curtailed the activities of those in central Europe.

DECLINE OF THE MEDIEVAL CHURCH

The period of the decline of the medieval Church may be dated 1305-1517. The first date marks the beginning of the Babylonian Captivity of the papacy about which we shall speak later; the latter is the year when Luther posted his theses on the church door at Wittenberg. There were many reasons for the decline of the papacy. First, there was the rise of national monarchs and the decline of feudalism; correspondingly there was a developing sense of nationality and increased loyalty of the people to their rulers. The Church claimed a supra-national loyalty which would certainly suffer with the spread of the new intense nationalism. On the other hand, as strong monarchs arose they became jealous of the immense wealth and power held by the Church within their borders. Second, the rigid enforcement of doctrine and practice, especially by means of the Inquisition, stirred up opposition and dissent. Third, the increasing cost of maintaining the hierarchy and the employment of oppressive means of securing money ostracized many. Fourth, there was an increasing moral laxity among churchmen, especially in the fifteenth century.

Fifth, this moral relaxation was accompanied by a general secularization of the Church during the fourteenth and especially the fifteenth century. Secularization of all of life was in process because of the Renaissance. The Renaissance was not just a re-birth of knowledge; it was a re-birth of the classical spirit, with its rationalistic outlook on life. The classical outlook had found its ethics by means of philosophy and therefore found them to be relativistic; it did not follow an unchangeable revealed standard. Moreover, the Renaissance marked the rise of the middle class with new wealth, which they commonly chose to spend on art, literature, education, and the like, rather than on the Church.

Sixth, the Crusades contributed in many ways to the decline of the Church. For instance, hordes of Europeans who had lived and died within sight of their lord's manor house, without education, bred on superstitions of the times, learned that life elsewhere was different. The new ideas and way of life with which they came in contact in the East weakened the ties of many to the Church. Last, the Babylonian Captivity of the Church and the Papal

Schism did much to weaken the power of Rome in Western Europe.

The Babylonian Captivity was a period of approximately seventy years (1305-1377) when the pope ruled from Avignon in Southern France. It was a time when the pope was virtual prisoner of the French king and when the papal interests were closely identified with French national interests. And during the captivity the Hundred Years War began between France and England, greatly weakening therefore the power of the papacy in England. During the war the pope demanded the surrender of Wycliffe, the great reformer; but the English parliament protected him. Moreover, the papacy became particularly debased during this period, disillusioning many.

The Papal Schism (1378-1417) hurt the papacy even more than the Babylonian Captivity. The schism resulted when the French and Italian cardinals could not agree on ending the Babylonian Captivity. So there was a split in the college of cardinals with the election of two popes— one at Rome and one at Avignon. When the Council of Pisa in 1409 tried to settle the problem, all it succeeded in doing was to elect a third pope; so for several years there were three popes anathematizing and excommunicating one another. Christendom was utterly confused. And reforming parties grew rapidly. It must be remembered that during this period Hus preached with great success in Bohemia, and the Lollards (followers of Wycliffe) secured a large following in England and Scotland.

Some have called the last part of the fifteenth century the paganized stage of the papacy. The Renaissance was taking its toll in the secularization of some of the top clergy. Nicholas V (1447-55) was a great lover of classical literature and the founder of the Vatican library. And Leo X (1513-21), the last pope before the Reformation, was very extravagant. As builder of St. Peter's in Rome, he used the revenues of the papacy on art, architecture, and the like. In fact, it should be remembered that his conflict with Luther came over the sale of indulgences—designed to raise money for the building of St. Peter's.

So at the beginning of the sixteenth century the medieval papacy was sick. But the disruption brought about by the Reformers stirred the Church to make changes which permitted a strong resurgence of power in later years.

Chapter VI

DISRUPTION OF THE HOLY CATHOLIC CHURCH

Long before Luther fired the verbal salvo against indulgences which began the Reformation, others had sniped at the theological position of the Roman Catholic Church. In fact, there had always been those within the Roman Church who did not agree with its teaching, and many had even broken away into separate religious communities.

FORERUNNERS OF THE REFORMATION

One of the most effective of the pre-Lutheran reformers was Peter Waldo, a wealthy merchant of Lyons, France. Putting great emphasis on the Scripture and scriptural methods, he translated portions of the Bible into the vernacular, stressed preaching even by laymen, and taught that the Roman Church was not infallible. At first Waldo had no intention of breaking with Rome, but in the latter part of the twelfth century the pope excommunicated him. After that he became more hostile to the Church. Taking a cue from the practice of Jesus, Waldo sent out seventy disciples to preach. The Waldenses spread into Southern France, Italy, Spain, and the Rhine Valley, and they may be found even today in Northern Italy. Perhaps it should be said that Waldo seems never to have become fully evangelical in the best sense of the term. But in pointing to the Scripture as the source of religious truth, he opened the door for his followers to become truly evangelical.

Like Peter Waldo, John Wycliffe (1320-84) was a Biblical reformer, bringing to bear the teachings of Scripture on the practices of the Roman Church. He also engaged in Bible translation, and it was through his efforts that the first English version was produced. While he personally translated or supervised translation of much of the Bible, his version was not completed until after his death. Sprung from a noble family, Wycliffe was educated at Oxford and later became master of Balliol College. He was, therefore, able to reach some of the upper class English. But he addressed himself largely to the common people, sending out lay evangelists to instruct them. Wycliffe opposed the infallibility of the pope, emphasized the invisible Church, and stressed the responsibility of the clergy to serve and help rather than to rule. For all of his efforts Gregory XI condemned him in 1377, but he was protected by Parliament. It is not clear how evangelical Wycliffe was personally, but under the influence of Biblical teaching his followers increasingly moved in that direction. Known as Lollards, Wycliffe's followers spread all over Britain and to the Continent. No doubt the Wycliffe movement helped to prepare the way for Lutheran and Calvinistic teachings when they invaded Britain centuries later.

Almost contemporary with Wycliffe was John Hus (1369-1415), professor of philosophy at the University of Prague. It is generally held that Hus was influenced by Wycliffe and that he simply adopted the views of Wycliffe as his own. However, recent scholarship has sought to pry Hus loose from such servile dependence and to claim that he developed much of his theology by himself. At any rate, his approach was similar to that of Wycliffe but his influence in Europe was much greater than that of the English leader. It should be remembered that Luther was greatly influenced by Hus, not by Wycliffe. Hus became the leader of a reform movement which spread across Bohemia. The whole nation supported him in his Church reform program, in spite of the fact that he was excommunicated by the pope. When the pope summoned Hus to the Council of Constance, the Emperor Sigismund ordered him to go and promised safe conduct to and from the Council. But when the Council condemned him as a heretic and burned him at the stake, Sigismund did not interfere. Like Luther, Hus came to blows with the pope over the issue of indulgences; but Europe was not so ready for the Reformation in 1415 as it was a century later.

One of the most remarkable figures in Europe during the latter part of the fifteenth century was Girolamo Savonarola (1452-98). A monk who became an itinerant preacher, Savonarola had his greatest ministry in Florence. There he led a reform movement; and in the midst of turbulent political conditions which resulted in the overthrow of the government of the city state, he became religious spokesman of the city with the opportunity of reforming it as he wished. He began to attack the corruption of the Church and the authority of the pope and to preach salvation apart from submission to the Roman hierarchy. This led Pope Alexander VI to interfere and ultimately to obtain Savonarola's condemnation and death sentence.

Contemporary with Savonarola there was a swarming of separatist groups that broke away from the Roman Church. These became more numerous and vocal during the days of Luther and Zwingli in the early sixteenth century, when the name Anabaptist was assigned to many of them. Anabaptist was a general term applied by Lutherans, Zwinglians, and Catholics to those who would not fellowship with any of these communions, who rejected a connection between Church and State, and who rejected infant baptism. Because the term Anabaptist was such a general descriptive, widely diverse views were held among them. Some were pantheistic, some extremely mystical, some anti-Trinitarian, some extreme millennialists, and some quite Biblical. Modern Baptists who like to place themselves in the Anabaptist tradition need to remember that comparatively few Anabaptists were truly Biblical. Furthermore, many of them, while they insisted on water baptism after a conversion experience, did not baptize by immersion. Moreover, the doctrinal position of Biblical Anabaptists is more closely related to the modern Mennonite viewpoint than to Baptist theology. Anabaptists were quite ascetic, tended to communism of goods, were pacifistic, opposed the use of oaths and capital punishment, and favored the free will of man as opposed to predestination.

Many other religious movements, for which there is no space here, spread across Europe during the fifteenth century, demonstrating how widespread was the demand for Church reform there. In fact, the continent was a seething kettle by 1500—ready to boil over. Economically, socially, politically, intellectually and religiously the time had come for an eruption. All that was needed was someone to mold these explosive elements into a single movement. Such a movement would blitz Europe. It was Martin Luther who gave direction to all of this explosive energy in what we now call the Protestant Reformation. For a clearer understanding of his place in the history of Europe, it is necessary to survey the various facets of life on the continent on the eve of the Reformation.

EUROPE ON THE EVE OF THE REFORMATION

In giving reasons for the decline of the papacy during the later Middle Ages, we have noted some of the properties on the stage of Europe while the drama of the

Reformation was enacted. Much more needs to be said on the subject.

Politically, the map of Europe was a crazy quilt composed of hundreds of principalities, evidencing extreme decentralization. But around the fringes, in Portugal, Spain, France, and England national states were rising, challenging the supra-national power of the papacy. In Central Europe Germany had an emperor checkmated by a number of states with slight allegiance to him. The Church possessed large German holdings, and the growth of many free cities further complicated the picture. Not only was the emperor hampered by his semi-independent vassals, but Mohammedan hosts knocked at the doors of the empire while Luther nailed his theses on the church door at Wittenberg. After toppling Constantinople and the Eastern Empire in 1453,[1] the Mohammedans advanced across Eastern Europe until they stood before the gates of Vienna in 1529. Harrassed by external and internal troubles, the emperor was not able to force Frederick of Saxony (one of his most powerful vassals) to surrender Luther.

Meanwhile Europe was expanding. A few years after Luther's birth, Columbus discovered the New World and launched the Spanish Empire in the West; shortly after Luther posted his theses, Magellan sailed around the world. At the same time the Portuguese were establishing outposts of empire in Brazil, Africa, and the Far East.

Intellectually, a new world of thought was discovered long before 1492. The full tide of the Renaissance had

---

[1] When Constantinople fell to the Mohammedan Turks, the center of power of the old Eastern Orthodox Church was destroyed. Thereafter the Orthodox Church broke up into national churches. For instance. the Russian bishops elected the head of the Church in Moscow as "Metropolitan of Moscow and all Russia." The national churches do not differ appreciably in theology and liturgy.

rolled in. Re-discovering the literature and thought patterns of the Classical Age, it had brought about a secularization of life. Humanism was one of the main features of the Renaissance, involving a new emphasis on man and his culture and making the world a better place in which man might live. The pull of the future life was not so great for the true child of the Renaissance as it had been for his forbears during the Middle Ages. He would rather eat his pie than have it in the sky by and by. In harking back to the literature of the Classical Age, the humanists put new emphasis on the study of Greek (and some of them Hebrew) in an effort to read the classics in the original. The greatest of all ancient documents was the Bible, and the renewed emphasis on ancient languages led many to the Scripture. The humanism of Northern Europe seemed to put more stress on the form and analysis of classical literature, while the humanism of Southern Europe seemed to stress the philosophy embedded in that literature. The literary humanists included a good deal of Biblical study in their academic diet; and it was in the North that the Reformation gained most headway. Zwingli, Calvin, and Erasmus are examples of the more Biblical of the literary humanists. Another important facet of the intellectual development of Europe at the time of the Reformation was the invention of movable type and the spread of printing.[2] Without it the Reformers could not have had the same effect. In fact, the tremendous literary activity of the Reformers was largely responsible for building the printing trade in many areas. Lastly, an important phenomenon of the Renaissance was the rise of universities, which provided

---

[2] Whether Coster or Gutenberg invented printing with movable type cannot be demonstrated with certainty, but the date was around 1430-40. The process was quite well developed during the latter part of the fifteenth century.

education for a larger number of people, fostered the critical spirit, and provided a means whereby the leaders of the new generation could be reached with Reformation principles and wherein they could be trained to promulgate them.

Religiously, Europe was in a condition of decay. The evils of the Church were many—simony, economic oppression, the purchase of salvation through indulgence traffic, immorality of many of the clergy, etc. The effects of the papal captivity and schism had been great, as noted earlier. The wave of secularism which engulfed Europe during the fifteenth century affected all levels of Church life: the parishioners, lower and higher clergy, monks, and even the successors of St. Peter.

Socially and economically, Europe was in a condition of unrest. Feudalism was on the decline, paralleled by the rise of towns and of nation states. This involved the emergence of a new middle class and a consequent social upheaval. Peasants were generally restless, looking for a way out of their economic and social oppression. Both national governments and the middle class had their eye on a ready supply of cash. Kings and nobles had to support armies and navies, finance public improvements, and promote the general welfare of their people. Businessmen needed to have capital reserve for new economic ventures. All this naturally hindered the flow of wealth to the Church; and efforts of the Church to drain money from an area were met with something less than enthusiasm by king and middle class alike.

THE REFORMATION IN GERMANY

To such an age as this, one seething with unrest and vexed with a host of problems and longings, came Martin Luther. He was a voice speaking for a multitude who had been voiceless. He was a leader who, many of the

disgruntled and striving forces of Europe hoped, would
guide them to a new freedom, success, and victory. Born
the son of a miner in 1483, Luther was well acquainted
with poverty. But he lived in a day when men were able
to better their fortunes; and Martin's father managed to
provide for him an early education. Thereafter, by his
own efforts and the help of friends, he attended the
University of Erfurt, where he earned the B. A. and M. A.
degrees.

The same year he received the M. A., he entered the
Augustinian monastery at Erfurt—apparently hoping to
find there the peace for his soul that he could not find
outside. Christ to him was a terrible judge. He spent
days in fasts and bodily mortification, seeking release for
his sinful soul. While in the monastery, he came under
the influence of Johann Von Staupitz who introduced
him to the love of God. Some claim that Luther was
converted at this time, but probably such was not the
case. Meanwhile Staupitz became dean and professor of
theology at the University of Wittenberg, and he arranged
for Luther to join the faculty of the university in 1508.
Two years later Luther went to Rome on a business trip
for the Augustinian order and had a chance to view the
papacy first hand; for him it was a disillusioning experience. When in 1512 he received his Doctor of Theology
degree, he succeeded Staupitz as professor of Theology,
which position he held until his death in 1546. He probably came to a real knowledge of the truth a few months
later as he taught Psalms and Romans. He was a Saul
turned Paul.

For several years he imparted his new-found peace to
his classes, but an opportunity for enlarged ministry came
in 1517. Albert, Archbishop of Mainz and holder of two
other high Church offices, made an arrangement with
Pope Leo X to raise money by the sale of indulgences,

half of which would go to pay the debts of Albert and the other half to help build St. Peter's Cathedral in Rome. The indulgence preachers at the time promised forgiveness of all sins to those who would contribute to the building of St. Peter's. Frederick of Saxony forbade the sale in his domain; so there was none of the traffic at Wittenberg. But Wittenberg citizens traveled to other towns to buy indulgences. This led Luther to post his famous Ninety-Five Theses on the church door at Wittenberg on October 31, 1517 in protest against the indulgence sale. Printed copies quickly flooded Europe, and popular enthusiasm was engendered everywhere. Luther even sent a copy to the Pope, for which he was ordered to appear in Rome for examination.

Nationalistically minded Frederic, ruler of Saxony, arranged for a meeting on German soil in 1518, which resulted in excommunication for Luther. In subsequent years the Pope repeatedly tried to get his hands on Luther, but he could not because Frederick protected him. The Emperor was loath to alienate Frederick because Saxony was the most powerful state in Germany at the time; and the Emperor needed all the support he could get for his war against the Turks. Finally in 1521, Luther went to the Diet of Worms under an imperial safe conduct. It was at Worms that he uttered the famous words: "I cannot and will not recant anything, since it is neither safe nor honest to act against one's conscience. God help me. Amen." On the way back Frederick's men kidnapped Luther to protect him and put him in the Wartburg Castle, where he worked on the translation of his New Testament into idiomatic German.[3] While there,

<hr>

[3] Luther used Erasmus' Greek Testament of 1516, the first printed Greek Testament, for his New Testament translation work. Later he translated the Old Testament. Luther's German Bible, because of its widespread use, was very significant in stand-

he was informed of extremism and violence at Wittenberg; so he returned to quell the disturbance.

During these years the Pope was still trying to stop Luther. At the Diet of Speyer (1529) it was resolved to forbid further spread of the Lutheran movement. Against this action *a protest* was entered by a number of German princes and free cities. From this the name Protestant passed on the whole movement. In the following year the Protestant princes got together in what was called the Schmalkald League. Already hard pressed by the Mohammedan Turks who appeared before the gates of Vienna in 1529, the Emperor Charles V granted freedom to the princes in 1532 and interfered no more for several years.

Meanwhile the Catholics became alarmed by the spread of Protestantism and banded together to form the Holy League. War broke out in 1546, the year Luther died. After initial victories by the Catholics, the Protestants finally pushed the imperial forces out of Germany. The Diet of Augsburg in 1555 ended the struggle and provided for a recognition of Catholicism and Lutheranism as legal religions in Europe.

Luther's right hand man at Wittenberg was Melanchthon, who directed the organizational, editorial, and publishing side of the Reformation. He is often called the teacher of Germany. He aided in establishing primary and secondary schools and did all he could to train the clergy. Recognizing the need of organizing the church which Luther had brought into being, he prepared a manual for that purpose. He also wrote a systematic theology, commentaries on New Testament books, and was largely responsible for preparing the various statements of faith

ardizing the German language—which at this time was spoken and written in many local dialects. Luther became to German what Dante was to Italian.

which the Lutherans presented at some of the diets where they met papal foes.

Luther was a popular and dynamic leader in an age that was looking for such leadership. He was an indefatigable critic of Romanism in an age that became increasingly critical of Romanism. He played on the national interests of the Germans in such pamphlets as his "Address to the Christian Nobles of the German Nation," in an age when nationalism was gathering momentum rapidly. He offered a message of hope and faith to a people lost in the darkness of sin and looking for light. For all of these reasons Luther was the success he became. But he has often been criticized because he did not go far enough in his reforms (he retained the crucifix, candles and other elements of Romanism) because he placed the Church under the control of civil authority, and because he failed to cooperate with the Swiss reformers and thus present a solid block of Protestants against Catholic power in Europe.

THE REFORMATION IN SWITZERLAND

Huldreich Zwingli (1484–1531) sparked the Reformation in German speaking Switzerland. After study at Bern, Vienna, and Basle, he was ordained and became parish priest at Glarus, where he remained for ten years. At Glarus he studied extensively the classics in the original languages, thus laying the foundation for his future Reformation work. In 1516 he moved to Einsiedeln for a three-year ministry. There he studied the Greek New Testament and began to found his preaching on the Gospel. Zwingli dated his arrival at evangelical truth to this period; thus his Reformation work began about the same time as Luther's. Since Einsiedeln was a religious center where an image of the Virgin was located, Zwingli had opportunity to preach to large groups against relics and mariolatry and about faith in Christ.

After becoming priest in a large cathedral in Zurich, Zwingli became more open about his views. He broke with the pope and married and preached openly against celibacy. Popular feeling was roused to such a point that the city council felt it necessary to appoint a public meeting for the discussion of religious subjects. When it convened, Zwingli presented his Sixty-Seven Articles and was so convincing that the council charged him to continue in evangelical methods and urged other preachers to follow his example. Tremendous changes followed; many priests married and set aside the mass. Some thought the evangelical movement had gone too far but the city council stood behind the Reformation and eventually abolished the mass and image worship altogether.

Gradually the Reformation triumphed in other cities of German Switzerland until the valley cantons were won. The forest or mountain cantons remained Catholic. Political tension heightened, the Protestants organizing a Christian Civic League and the Catholics organizing also and forming an alliance with Ferdinand of Austria. War broke out in 1529 and ended early in 1531; the Protestants were defeated and Zwingli was slain. Thereafter the Reformation program in German Switzerland was on the defensive; some ground was regained after Calvin came on the scene.

As has been indicated, Zwingli directed the Reformation in Switzerland along civic lines with a view to establishing a model Christian community. He persuaded the city council to legislate the various details of the Reformation and to supervise the carrying out of their decisions. In other words, he aimed at political as well as spiritual regeneration.

Zwingli's theology put great emphasis on the sovereignty

of God and His election unto salvation. He held that the Lord's Supper contributed nothing to the elect; it was merely a symbol or remembrance of the sacrifice of Christ. In this he could not agree with Luther who held that the body and blood of Christ are really present in the communion. This was the rock on which the negotiations of the German and Swiss Reformers broke at Marburg in 1529. The Zwinglian movement merged into Calvinism later in the sixteenth century.

John Calvin (1509–64) is often called the Patrician of the Reformation. His family had been artisans and had good economic and political connections. Calvin started out in the Church but was never ordained to the priesthood; his father wanted him to study law and he did for a while. He studied at Paris, Orleans, and Bourges. At the latter university he came under the influence of Wolmar, with whom he studied Greek and Hebrew and the New Testament in the original. His conversion dated sometime during 1532 or 1533. Calvin says his conversion was sudden, through private study, and because he failed to find peace in absolutions, penances, and intercessions of the Church. After that he resigned his Church offices and later was thrown into prison for some of his evangelical activities in Paris.

On release he became a refugee and moved around a good deal in Germany and Switzerland. During this period in his life Calvin came in contact with Martin Bucer, the great reformer of Strasburg, who was professor of theology at the university there. And at Basel in 1536, at the age of only twenty-six, he published the first edition of his *Institutes of the Christian Religion*. The last edition in 1559 was about three times the size of the original. Later in 1536 Calvin decided that after paying a last visit to his native France he would settle down in Strasburg.

But he passed through Geneva on the way and there

William Farel persuaded Calvin to remain and help him with the Reformation there. In 1535 Geneva officially became Protestant. And the city council had made laws against drunkenness, gambling, dancing, and the like; but the laws had little effect.[4] So when Calvin came he prepared a catechism, articles of faith, and insisted on the right of the Church to exercise discipline over unworthy communicants. Farel and Calvin exercised great authority in Geneva 1536–38, working hard to establish the community on a theocratic basis. But the population was not ready for the rigid discipline; so Farel and Calvin were banished and went to Strasburg. Finally in 1541, when conditions in Geneva became critical, the people begged them to return. They did reluctantly. And for the rest of his life Calvin worked tirelessly in his adopted city.

During those years Church and state were closely linked in Geneva, and it is obvious from a comparison of the Institutes and actual historical development that the Church at Geneva had far less freedom than Calvin believed was right. His system of representative government is more adequately seen in the Church of Scotland.

John Calvin was probably the most influential leader of the Reformation era. He put much stress on education. His catechetical system for the young has been carried all over the world. And at his College of Geneva were trained men who spread Presbyterianism all over Western Europe. It was Calvin's theology and form of Church government that triumphed in the Protestant Church of France, the Reformed Church of Germany, the Church of Scotland, the Reformed Church in Hungary, the Reformed Church

---

[4] Thus it can be seen that Calvin was not responsible for the stringent code of conduct imposed upon citizens of Geneva during his ministry there; it antedated him. Therefore he should not be blamed for it.

in Holland, and in Puritanism in Old and New England.[5] Lutheranism, on the other hand, won only part of Germany, Scandinavia, and influenced the English and American picture. Calvin's Biblical and theological writings have also been very influential. And Calvin is called the father of the historical grammatical method of Biblical study—a method which attempts to discover what the Scripture meant to those who wrote it, and what it means according to the common definition of its words.

The Reformation in France

As already noted, Protestantism in France followed Calvin in doctrine and government—after a brief initial impact of Lutheranism. Protestantism entered France in the days of Francis I, who never seems to have followed a consistent attitude toward it. He was Catholic in Paris and Protestant in the provinces. Under his successor, Henry II (1547–59) the same policy was followed. And by his death the Huguenots, as the French Protestants were called, numbered perhaps as many as 400,000.

When Henry died, he left behind him young sons who were dominated by his queen Catherine de' Medici and her uncles of the Guise family. This raised problems in France because the Guises were strongly Catholic and, coming from Lorraine, were looked on by many of the French nobility as foreigners. Moreover, many of the nobles of France were greatly opposed to the crown, not only because they felt that the crown was too autocratic but because they were jealous of their ancient family rights. The House of Bourbon and the House of Chatillon were two of the leading opponents of the crown and the

---

[5] Puritanism adopted the Congregational form of church government but retained Calvinistic theology.

Guises. Not only were they opposed on the grounds previously mentioned, but their heads were Protestant as well.

Such animosities provided the tinder to ignite armed conflict. In fact eight wars were fought between Catholic and Protestant forces in France. Leading the Protestant forces early in the conflict was Gaspard de Coligny of the House of Chatillon. But he lost his life along with tens of thousands of other Protestants in the massacre of St. Bartholomew's Day, August 24, 1572 at the instigation of Catherine de' Medici. Thereafter Henry of Navarre, of the Bourbon family, took the lead of the Protestants. His military activities were successful; and ultimately, with the death of others in the royal line, he became heir to the throne of France. Since he did not have quite enough strength to complete his conquest, he turned Catholic and won the crown. Judging from his conduct, Henry's religious principles sat rather lightly on his shoulders. His switch to catholicism was obviously for political reasons, and perhaps to turn off the blood bath that was drenching France.

At any rate, in 1598 Henry published the Edict of Nantes, an edict of toleration for the Huguenots. It guaranteed them the right to hold public office, freedom of worship in most areas of France, and the privilege of educating their children in other than Roman Catholic schools. Though they enjoyed a period of great prosperity, the Huguenots became a defensive minority, and finally Louis XIV revoked the edict in 1685. Thousands were driven into exile to the benefit of England, Holland, Prussia, and America.

THE REFORMATION IN ENGLAND

The marital problems of Henry VIII sparked the Reformation in England. Not only was he tired of Catherine of Aragon and enamored with Anne Boleyn, but he was concerned over the fact that Catherine had not provided him with a male heir. This could well have lead to civil war after Henry's death. So Henry sought annulment of his marriage at the hands of the Pope. But Clement VII, under the influence of the powerful Charles V of Spain would not agree. In the midst of the struggle Henry managed to install Thomas Cranmer as Archbishop of Canterbury and to win from him annulment of his marriage to Catherine. In 1534 Parliament passed the Supremacy Act, making Henry head of the Church of England. Soon thereafter Henry, in need of money and afraid of a fifth column in the realm, closed the monasteries of England. It should be remembered that Henry did not provide a Protestant theology for England; he merely changed the headship of the English Church.

There was a marked change, however, during the reign of Edward VI (1547–53). Coming to the throne at a very early age, he was ruled by older men who were of Protestant persuasion. The liturgy was changed, services conducted in English, a prayer book composed, marriage allowed for the clergy, and the mass and images done away. Archbishop Cranmer and others composed the Forty-Two Articles, which later became the Thirty-Nine Articles of the Church of England. The Articles, basically Lutheran in viewpoint, were subscribed to by the King but not the Parliament.

Edward died in the midst of a Catholic reaction. So when Mary (1553–58) took the throne as a Catholic, she was well received. In 1554 she married Philip of Spain and thereafter spent little time in the country. While Edward's religious policy had been too sudden in one direction, Mary's was too strong in the other. In fact, Mary brought the English Church once more within the Roman fold. Many Protestants fled the country; some 300 were martyred, including such outstanding leaders as Cranmer, Ridley, and Latimer.

The reign of Elizabeth I (1558–1603) was well received by the English people. Persecution came to an end, as did the threat of Spanish interference. The Church of England was re-established, a prayer book drawn up, and the Forty-Two Articles revised to Thirty-Nine and adopted by Parliament. Queen Elizabeth loved an ornate service and under her influence the Church of England developed its liturgy in that direction.

In this she was opposed by the Puritans. The Puritans, who are known to have existed as early as the days of Edward, were long on Calvinism, rigid morals, and church discipline and short on ritualism. They also favored representative government as opposed to the episcopal form of the Church of England. Also opposing Elizabeth were the Independents or Congregationalists who came into existence during her reign. They held to complete separation of church and state and a congregational form of government. About the end of Elizabeth's reign the Baptists appeared, drawing members from the ranks of the Puritans and Congregationalists. They differed from the Congregationalists as to mode of baptism and as to persons who were proper candidates for baptism. Baptists accepted only baptism by immersion after a conversion experience.

James VI of Scotland became James I of England in 1603 and is significant to Church history for his interest in the version which bears his name. James is also important because he increased the opposition of the Puritans to the crown by arranging for Sunday sports and by encouraging Arminianism in England. This animosity grew, until in the days of Charles I, it erupted in civil war (1642–46). From 1640 to 1660 Parliament and Oliver Cromwell ruled the nation. The Puritan divines worked with the Commissioners of the Church of Scotland to compose the Westminster Confession, which was adopted by the Church of Scotland in 1647 and in part by the English Parliament in 1648.

THE REFORMATION IN SCOTLAND

Probably in no country of Europe were the Catholic clergy more depraved than in Scotland at the time of the Reformation. This fact, taken in conjunction with remaining influences of Wycliffe and the old Celtic Church, and the infiltration of Lutheran ideas, greatly contributed to the rise of the Reformation in Scotland.

The pioneer Reformer in Scotland was Patrick Hamilton who had gone to Wittenberg to study with Luther and had returned to his homeland to preach. He was burned as a heretic in 1528. The second great leader of the Scottish Reformation was George Wishart, who had a Zwinglian and Calvinistic background. Wishart was martyred in 1546. Martyrs' blood stirred many a heart in Bonnie Scotland.

Wishart's most ardent follower was John Knox—a leader with all the enthusiasm and popular power of Luther and the steadfastness of Calvin. After university training at Glasgow, Knox went to serve as chaplain at St. Andrews Castle, a Protestant center. A French fleet took the castle and sold Knox as a galley slave. After nineteen months the English rescued him, and he ministered in England during the days of Edward VI. Leaving England when Mary Tudor (Bloody Mary) came to the throne, he went to Geneva to study with Calvin. Meanwhile the Reformation message spread widely among the common people and found ready acceptance. Many nobles also became Protestants. Knox was invited to return to Scotland in 1559 and immediately went to work organizing the Church of Scotland. He and some associates drew up a statement of faith and a statement of Church government, both of which were approved by Parliament. The first general assembly of the Church met in 1560.

It should be remembered that after the death of James V in 1542 Scotland was ruled by his wife, Mary of Guise, of a noble French family and virtually a tool of the French. Her daughter, Mary, when six years old, was sent to France for education where she was married to the Dauphin. Mary of Guise even had French troops stationed in Scotland. Many of the nobles, both because they were Protestants and good Scots, banded together to expel the French. In this they were aided by an English fleet. The French were defeated in 1560.

Mary came back to Scotland in 1561—without the Dauphin who had died. She was beautiful and winsome. One after another of the Protestant nobles fell for her wiles, even though she was determined to force Catholicism on Scotland. Ultimately, however, she alienated both Protestants and Catholics from her by her love affairs with worthless men. And in a brief civil war she was captured and forced to abdicate in favor of her infant son James VI. Later Mary was beheaded by Elizabeth for treason.

Protestantism was definitely established by Parliament. Knox had done his work. His impress may still be seen on the Church of Scotland and the educational system of the land. When he died in 1572, Andrew Melville took over his work and perfected the system he established.

THE REFORMATION IN THE NETHERLANDS

The teachings of Luther and especially of Calvin were readily accepted in the Netherlands. And the great humanist Erasmus did much of his work there, writing devastating satires on the Roman Church under the titles of *The Praise of Folly* and *Familiar .Colloquies*. Moreover, the Bible had been translated into Flemish several years before Luther was born.

Spain controlled the Netherlands during the Reformation, and it was the great Charles V who first had to deal with Protestants. There were many martyrdoms in his days, especially of Anabaptists. But the real inquisition was engineered by Philip II (1555–98). Both political and religious resentment arose as a result of Philip's actions. In the midst of a famine, Spanish troops were quartered in the land. At the same time he pushed through a plan to create many new bishoprics to provide more machinery for the Inquisition. In 1566 Protestant nobles met and signed a league to resist the despotic rule of Philip. Shortly thereafter a wave of iconoclasm swept over the country and many churches were looted. This gave Philip the excuse he was looking for. He instituted a terrible inquisition.

Meanwhile William of Orange organized armed resistance by Dutch patriots. Though the Dutch did not seem to be very successful on land, they did fairly well on the sea. There they had the help of a navy which Elizabeth provided. Though William was assassinated in 1584, the Dutch were able to expel the last of the Spanish in 1609 and to win independence officially in 1648 with the Peace of Westphalia. The Reformed Church was officially established in the Netherlands.

THE COUNTER REFORMATION

The Counter Reformation launched by the Roman Church was successful for several reasons: 1. Protestants lost their early evangelical enthusiasm. 2. The controversial spirit grew among Protestants. 3. The papacy had the advantage of a thoroughly organized system. 4. The papacy was supported by Romance peoples—among whom there was little reformation. 5. The Roman Church profited by the Reformation and set its house in order somewhat.

There are three aspects to the Counter Reformation. The first of these was the Council of Trent. During Luther's ministry there was constant agitation for and promise of a council to deal with the issues that the Reformation had raised. The Council of Trent was that council. It met in a total of twenty-five sessions under three popes over the years 1545 to 1563. The Council decided a host of issues including the validity of the seven sacraments in bestowing merit on the believer and the necessity of some of them for salvation, the value of tradition as a basis of authority alongside the Bible, the canonicity of the apocryphal books of the Old Testament, the existence of purgatory, and the value of invocation of saints, images, relics, and indulgences. The Council issued a statement of faith by which a true Catholic could determine his orthodoxy. No such comprehensive statement existed before. If it had, perhaps the force of the Reformation would have been blunted in some places.

The Inquisition was another feature of the Counter Reformation. The medieval Inquisition, discussed earlier, was revived during the sixteenth century, especially in Italy and Spain and her dependencies. Though the Netherlands was subjected to a terrible persecution, Protestantism triumphed there. But in Italy and Spain the Inquisition was fairly successful in extirpating the effects of the Reformation. Dominicans usually served as inquisitorial officers.

The Jesuits were the third aspect of the Counter Reformation. The order was founded in Paris in 1534 by Ignatius Loyola. The order demanded slavish obedience of all its members for the furtherance of the interests of the Roman Church. They were absolutely unscrupulous in their methods, holding that it was permissible to do evil if good might come of it. The Inquisition could win back individuals where the Reformation had slight effect. In other areas the Jesuits set up schools to convert the minds of the populace, sought to infiltrate governmental office, or use every means fair or foul to advance the cause of the Church. Their power became so great and their methods so immoral that the order was even suppressed by the papacy 1773–1814.

THE THIRTY YEARS WAR

The Reformation period closed with a blood bath that is known as the Thirty Years War. The struggle began in Bohemia after several years of agitation between Catholics and Calvinists. In 1618 the Bohemians refused to recognize the newly elected Catholic Emperor Ferdinand II and elected Frederick V of the Palatinate of Germany, a Calvinist, as their king. This could only lead to open warfare. The war can be divided into four stages: 1618–23 when the Catholics were victorious and crushed Protestantism in Bohemia, Moravia, and Austria; 1623–29 when the war took on an all-European character and the Catholics again defeated the Protestants under the leadership of Christian IV of Denmark; 1630–32 when the Catholics were disunited and the Protestants made a comeback under Gustavus Adolphus, the "Lion of the North"; 1632–48 when the war became a struggle for political advantage between the various powers of Europe. Finally the war ended with the Peace of Westphalia in 1648 which recognized Catholicism, Calvinism, and Lutheranism as legal religions. The religion of the prince was to be that of the people, according to the status of an area in 1624. This meant that Protestantism was estab-

lished in England, Scotland, Holland, Scandinavia, part of
Germany and part of Switzerland.

In reply to those who criticize Christianity for the
many wars it fought during the Reformation period, it
must be observed that in every case political, economic,
and social considerations were factors often as important
as the religious. Much of the time there was no clear-cut
struggle between Catholics and Protestants. Let it be
remembered that both Protestants and Catholics were
found in the armies which opposed Mary Queen of Scots.
The Reformer Henry of Navarre was supported in his
bid for the throne of France both by Protestants and
Catholics. And during much of the Thirty Years War
Catholic France was allied with Protestant Sweden.

Chapter VII

EUROPE IN THE MODERN ERA

The Seventeenth Century

THE SEVENTEENTH CENTURY was a century of orthodoxy. It was a time during which Protestantism and Catholicism were concerned with dogmatic formulation of their positions for the purpose of catechizing their adherents. While some of this orthodoxy stressed Christian experience, much of it emphasized right thinking. The drying up of the wellsprings of vitality in religion had begun by the beginning of the seventeenth century, but the process was hastened in certain areas of Europe which lay prostrate as a result of the Thirty Years War. Cold orthodoxy will not long satisfy. It will produce at least three reactions or results: rationalism, Biblical revivalism, or extreme forms of mysticism. In other words, some will substitute reason; others will return to a healthy combination of doctrine and experience; still others will substitute the authority of experience for the authority of creeds and catechisms.

Prominent among the inner light or mystical groups of the seventeenth century were the Quakers. Originator of the movement was George Fox of Drayton, England. Following a religious experience in 1646, he began a forty-year ministry of itinerant preaching. Quakerism spread very rapidly across England and after its organization in 1660, to the Continent, Asia, Africa, the West Indies and North America. There William Penn founded a haven for them in Pennsylvania in 1682. The Quakers were severely persecuted, not only because of their great difference from the confessional churches on many points but because of their open criticism of others. Quakerism emphasized the work of the Holy Spirit: that the revelations of the Spirit or the inner light were superior to the Bible but not contradictory to it; that since the Holy Spirit speaks to all, special training and ministers were unnecessary; that the Spirit could speak through women as well as men; and that formal worship was an abomination to God. They did not practice the sacraments nor take oaths or do military service.

The great Swedish scientist, Emanuel Swedenborg (1688–1772) was responsible for founding the New Jerusalem Church. He claimed to have had a revelation which enabled him to communicate with the world of spirits and angels; and during his various communications with that world he claimed to have learned the secrets of the universe. Instead of rejecting the Bible, he spiritualized or allegorized it. The theological system he developed had some similarities to Gnosticism. Swedenborgian churches were established in Sweden, England, Germany, and in many places in North America.

Within Romanism there was also a reaction to the rationalization of dogma, which expressed itself in an extreme mystical movement. Known as Quietism, it held that God can act on man to meet his spiritual need only as man surrenders himself utterly. When man's soul is completely passive, the way is open to receive impartation of divine light from God. Some of the Quietists were pantheistic in approach—teaching that a contemplation of the Divine would lead to absorption into the Divine. Michael Molinos, Madame Guyon, and Francis Fenelon were three of Quietism's leading writers. A contemporary Roman Catholic reaction which stressed experience, though not of the same type, was Jansenism. So named from its leader Cornelis Jansen, it sought to return to the teachings of Augustine and to stress greater personal holiness and the necessity of divine grace for conversion.

A seventeenth century evangelical corrective to the cold orthodoxy of the Lutheran Church was Pietism. While its main center was in Germany, it claimed many adherents in Switzerland and Holland as well. In Holland the revolt was against the Dutch Reformed Church. Pietism emphasized the need for a regeneration experience on the part of all, promoted a living Christianity wherein the love of God would be expressed, and encouraged practical Church work and Bible study on the part of laymen. The great leaders of German Pietism were P. J. Spener and A. H. Francke; the latter was especially important for his training schools at Halle.

While Pietism reacted primarily against Lutheranism, Arminianism reacted against the Reformed Church of Holland. Calvinism in Holland had grown much more harsh and severe than it was in Calvin's day. So the Arminians in 1610 (a year after the death of Jacobus Arminius their leader) addressed a *Remonstrance* to the States of Holland. In it they emphasized the opportunity and responsibility of man in salvation: that man faces alternate choice of salvation or condemnation and is actually free, that predestination is conditioned on God's foreknowledge of man's faith and perseverance, that while grace is indispensable it is not irresistible, and that to stay saved man must desire God's help and be actively engaged in living the Christian life. Perhaps it should be noted that both Arminianism and Calvinism have over the centuries grown more extreme than the views set forth by their founders. Much misunderstanding of both positions and much quibbling between groups holding these divergent positions could be stopped if there

were a wider reading and understanding of the works of
Calvin and Arminius.

One of the more important rationalistic movements
of the seventeenth century was Socinianism, so named
for its founder Faustus Socinus (1539–1604). Coming
originally from Italy, Socinus spent most of his years of
teaching and preaching in Poland. There he set forth an
essentially anti-Trinitarian system. He taught that Christ
was a man who lived a life of exemplary obedience and
ultimately was deified. One becomes a Christian by following Christ's example of devotion to God, renuncia-
tion of the world and humility. Christ's death was not
substitutionary but merely an example of ultimate devotion. After a couple of generations of success in Poland,
the Socinian movement was broken up by the Jesuits and
its followers banished. Many of them found their way to
Holland where they were welcomed by Arminians and
others and where they injected a considerable liberal
influence into the theology of the country. From there
Socinian influence also spread into the Church of England.

THE EIGHTEENTH CENTURY

If the seventeenth century was the age of orthodoxy,
the eighteenth was the age of rationalism. In part, rationalism was a reaction to or an outgrowth of cold orthodoxy. And in part it grew out of the great emphasis on
faith and emotion during the seventeenth century. Many
of the groups which stressed experience did not strive
hard enough to meet the intellectual needs of their con-
stituency. In their emphasis on emotion they neglected
a doctrinal basis of their faith. Note for instance that
Immanuel Kant, a watershed in the history of philosophy,
was the son of Pietistic parents and that he was educated
as a Pietist until 1740. The rise of rationalism was also

due to the place given to philosophy in the universities. During the Middle Ages philosophy and theology had been wed in the system called Scholasticism; but with the decline of Scholasticism and the Church the two were divorced, with the result that philosophy became an enemy of theology.

Furthermore, the rise of rationalism was due to scientific developments. Copernicus (1473–1543) was responsible for developing the view that the sun instead of the earth was the center of the universe. Galileo (1546–1642) trained the telescope on the heavens and used observation to support Copernicus' view of the solar system. Descartes (1596–1650) and Isaac Newton (1642–1727) propounded the concept of a universe governed by natural law. Francis Bacon (1561–1626) introduced the inductive method or the scientific method, according to which the scientist accepted nothing on the basis of authority alone but developed his theories by observing phenomena. So knowledge was tied to what the senses could discover, and the result was a materialistic approach to life. Revelation tended to take the back seat to reason and knowledge gained by sense perception.

Natural theology rather than revealed theology became fashionable. And the religious philosophy of deism won the minds of many of the upper classes in Europe and America. This was the view that God created the solar system and then sent it whirling off into space under the control of natural law; He does not now interfere in the affairs of the universe. So revelation contained in a Bible or in Christ, providence, or prayer have no place in one's religious system. The Bible does, however, contain ethical laws which serve as guideposts for a moral life glorifying to God.

Keeping step with the rise of deism was the development of a new social philosophy. John Locke (1632–

1704) taught that just as the universe was governed by natural law, so men were guaranteed certain natural rights. His philosophy was basic to the thought of the eighteenth century. Voltaire (1694–1778) and Rousseau (1712–1778) broadened Locke's views and popularized them in France, where they were adopted by the revolutionaries. And in America Jefferson wrote Locke's philosophy into the Declaration of Independence.

The social philosophers or Philosophes, as they were called, thought that just as man could discover the laws of nature and bend it to the service of man, so man could discover the laws of society and remake it into a more equitable and reasonable structure. In doing so, they held that the "rubbish" of the past which impeded man's progress had to go. One important part of that debris was the Church. And the Church in France meant the Catholic Church. After its disestablishment, the goddess of reason was enthroned in Paris. By the time of the Revolution many of the deists of the days of Voltaire and Rousseau saw no need for a God to set their world going and many turned atheists. Deism made great inroads in England, France, Germany, and other countries of Europe, as well as in America.

Attack and counter-attack are characteristic both of the eighteenth and nineteenth centuries. Forces at work during the nineteenth century are discussed later. The attack during the eighteenth century was made by rationalism; a counter-attack was launched by such groups as Moravians and Methodists. The Moravian movement was an outgrowth of Pietism. Its leader, Count Zinzendorf, had spent several years in one of the schools at Halle. Zinzendorf in 1722 invited exiled Protestants from Bohemia and Moravia to settle on his estate in Saxony, where he organized the "renewed fraternity." He developed a very keen interest in world evangelization, but he was especially concerned with developing an international fellowship of true believers belonging to various religious bodies. He did not want to start a new denomination. His own colony he kept within the Lutheran Church. Other fellowships soon sprang up in Holland, Denmark, England, North America, and elsewhere in Germany. Later Zinzendorf grew at odds with the Lutheran Church and the government of Saxony and was exiled for over ten years; during this period the Moravian community organized as the Unity of the Brethren in 1742. The name Moravian was applied to the group in England.

The Moravians had a direct influence in the establishment of the Methodist movement. It was Moravian missionaries who exposed the Wesleys to the Gospel message as the latter returned from a missionary journey to the New World. Methodist was the name applied to the "holy club" at Oxford to which the Wesleys and George Whitefield belonged; thereafter it passed on to the movement begun by the three. John Wesley and George Whitefield were the great preachers; Charles Wesley was the hymn writer, having composed over 6000—he is ranked by some as the greatest hymn writer of all ages.[1] As the Wesleys carried on their revival efforts, they received little encouragement from the Anglican Church of which they were members. Shut out of many Anglican Churches, they took a cue from Whitefield who had had great success in outdoor preaching in America. Tremendous crowds constantly gathered for their meetings.

Early Methodism was characterized by the preaching of present assurance of salvation, attainableness of Christian perfection in this life, and a dignified ritual. The

---

[1] Charles Wesley was contemporary with another great hymn writer, Isaac Watts (1674-1748). John Newton (1725-1807) began his hymn writing ministry as Wesley was passing off the scene.

Wesleys were Arminian in their theology, but Whitefield was Calvinistic.[2] Originally, John Wesley did not wish to organize the Methodist Church as a separate denomination; he set up societies within the Anglican Church. But conditions in America demanded a separation, and the Methodist Episcopal Church was established in 1784. In England, Methodism separated from the Anglican Church around 1800.

As well as having a wide spiritual impact, Methodism proved to be a very real answer to the social ills of the day. Spiritually, Methodism was the answer to deism in England, especially among the lower and middle classes. And it met the needs of the new laboring classes in the cities, for whom the Anglican Church did not assume much responsibility. Socially it, in large measure retarded forces which in France led to the Revolution, provided poor relief, medical dispensaries, orphanages, and was at the front of the movement for prison reform and the abolition of slavery.

THE NINETEENTH CENTURY

If the seventeenth century may be characterized as the age of orthodoxy and the eighteenth as the age of rationalism, then the nineteenth may be characterized as the age of science. But science takes over after the middle of the century; other forces were at work in the early part of the century. The Enlightenment of the eighteenth century had gone too far in its effort to eradicate religion and to remove feeling from all of life. The first part of the nineteenth century saw a reaction to that extreme in what is called Romanticism. Romanticism was characterized by a new emphasis on feeling in all phases of life, by a renewed interest in religion, and by an organic

---

[2] Calvinistic Methodists are most numerous in Wales today.

view of history and society. In other words, the social structure could not be torn up and made over as the Philosophes thought; it was subject to slow and gradual change. The present has an organic connection with the past.

In the wake of the Romantic Reaction, there was revival of religion of all types. The Roman Church was re-established under Napoleon. A stained-glass view of the Middle Ages replaced that of the black-shrouded view painted by the Philosophes. Schleiermacher in Germany re-defined religion as feeling—a feeling of dependence on God as man comes to realize how finite, limited, and temporary he is in comparison with the eternal principle indwelling the world. Schleiermacher's rationalized Christianity has influenced such recent movements as Neo-Orthodoxy and Existentialism.

An evangelical revival moved through the Church of England during the first third of the century under the leadership of such well-known saints as John Newton and William Wilberforce.[3] Meanwhile Methodist, Baptist and other dissenter groups grew rapidly in number. The Sunday School movement spread across England like a prairie fire, and several Bible Societies were founded in Europe and America—including the British and Foreign Bible Society, the Berlin Bible Society, and the American Bible Society. Meanwhile, the foreign missions movement continued to expand. In fact the nineteenth century has been called the "Great Century of Protestant Missions."

The modern missionary movement actually began with William Carey (1761–1834) whose efforts led to the

---

[3] This evangelical party is known as the Low-Church party. There is in the Anglican Church also a High-Church party, Anglo-Catholic in sentiment, and the Broad-Church party, which seeks to take the middle way of compromise and make Anglicanism the Church of the nation.

founding of the Baptist Missionary Society at Kettering, England, in 1792. The following year Carey set out for India. As reports of his work reached home, members of other denominations banded together to form the London Missionary Society in 1792. Other societies followed in rapid succession. Carey taught himself several languages of India and became a leader in Bible translation. He was followed there by the Anglican Henry Martyn and the Church of Scotland's Alexander Duff. Samuel Marsden pioneered for over forty years in Australia, New Zealand, and the Pacific Islands. The London Missionary Society sent Robert Morrison to open up the work in China and Robert and Mary Moffat and David Livingstone to Africa. Morrison provided the Chinese dictionary and Chinese translation of the Bible for later missionaries there. Moffat translated the Bible into important tribal languages of South Africa. Livingstone opened up Central Africa. In 1865 J. Hudson Taylor founded the China Inland Mission, one of the great interdenominational faith missions.

England and Scotland were not the only European countries sending out missionaries during the nineteenth century. In 1821 the Basel Evangelical Missionary Society and Danish Missionary Society were founded. Three years later, in 1824, the Berlin Missionary Society and the Paris Missionary Society came into being.

Although the beginnings of the scientific revolution can be traced back to the sixteenth century, science did not make its full impact on society until the nineteenth century. It was the harnessing of technology and science that changed the way men lived. While the factory system began to re-shape the English countryside during the eighteenth century and to herd masses of humanity into foreboding aggregations called cities, the industrial revolution was not so widespread in other countries until the nineteenth century. Moreover, the number of new inventions that suddenly changed human existence and accelerated the growth of cities came around the middle of the nineteenth century and later.

As people moved into the cities, they found a hard lot indeed. Whole families worked for a pittance from dawn to dark in factories without safety devices, and they lived in impossible tenements. Their interest in life was making a living—keeping body and soul together. Much of their interest was centered in organizations that would better their lot. As unions and governmental agencies took over functions and provided social outlet previously furnished by the Church, society became increasingly secularized. Materialism overspread all things. Sunday was the workers' day off, and they used it as a day for recreation. Had they wanted to go to church in many cities, there would not have been enough for them to go to as denominations often failed keep up with the need. It may be said that the real enemy of religion was the science of the shop rather than the science of the laboratory.

Yet the impact of the science of the laboratory was tremendous. The publication of Darwin's *Origin of the Species* in 1859 culminated a long history of evolution. Now man was no longer the creature of God but the product of an infinite process of development necessitated by the demands of environment; he marked the survival of the fittest. Mind had been banished from the universe; there was no longer any need for God. The reaction of established religion to Darwinism was threefold: some capitulated and turned their backs on Christianity; others repudiated the claims of science; the majority worked out some sort of compromise between their faith and the new science.

Not only did the concept of evolution invade the field of science but of religion as well. It was commonly taught that man started out with no religion and finally advanced to the elevated viewpoint of monotheism. The Bible was not a product of revelation, but a collection of myths, legends and a few historical facts which developed over the years and finally was edited and put in the form we now know it. The Tubingen and Wellhausen Schools of thought were two of those that subscribed to the evolutionary and higher critical viewpoint in religion.

But conservative forces were at work also. In Romanism a powerful battle was waged against higher criticism, and Pius IX at the Vatican Council of 1870 succeeded in foisting on the Church the dogma of papal infallibility in an effort to control Catholicism more effectively. In Germany such great scholars as Hengstenberg and Franz Delitzsch made their impact. In England Booth organized the Salvation Army; George Williams started the YMCA; John Darby initiated the Plymouth Brethren movement; the Anglican Church launched the Church Army; and the revival efforts of Moody and Sankey were quite effective. In Holland, Abraham Kuyper founded the Free University of Amsterdam, destined to become a great center of orthodoxy. In short, throughout Western Europe there were individuals and groups who landed telling blows against the bastions of anti-supernaturalism. And it would take pages to list the Spirit-sent revivals that fell on England and the Continent during the century.

Chapter VIII

THE CHURCH IN AMERICA

The Seventeenth Century and Before

WHEN COLUMBUS SAILED WESTWARD in 1492, he was not merely looking for a new route to the Indies. He hoped to discover new sources of wealth to finance another crusade against the Mohammedans. And when he came upon the heathen tribes of the New World, his religious inclinations predominated again. He and Ferdinand agreed that measures should be taken to protect, convert and civilize the Indians. Promptly Spanish priests were sent out with the explorers and conquerors. A bishopric was established at Santo Domingo in 1512, another in Cuba in 1522, with others following in rapid succession. The University of Mexico was founded in 1551 and the University of Lima in 1557; others were built elsewhere in Latin America as the need arose. It will be clear that these institutions were primarily for the civilization of the natives when one recalls that the Spanish sent their sons back to Europe for education. Admittedly the Spanish oppressed and maltreated the Indians over the centuries, but it is nevertheless true that the Church and Crown made sincere and expensive moves to protect the natives. Shortly after the death of Luther, the Spanish settled Florida and then advanced into New Mexico and Texas. They were establishing their missions in California while Jefferson was writing the Declaration of Independence. Portuguese settlement in Brazil began in 1510, and of course the Roman Church was established there. Thus all of Latin America and part of the present area of the United States responded to the religious efforts of Spanish and Portuguese priests.

While the French became interested in North America very early, they were not able to establish a permanent colony until 1608—at Quebec. Thereafter French explorers and missionaries ranged across the North and throughout the Mississippi Valley down to its mouth in Louisiana. They set up mission stations across Canada and built up a friendship with many Indian tribes. But the paucity of French settlers in the New World and inadequate colonial policies ultimately brought an end to the French Empire in North America and the effects of French Jesuit work everywhere except in Quebec and Louisiana.

At Jamestown in 1607 the English established their first successful colony. Planted by the Virginia Company, the colony was basically an economic and colonizing venture; but the Anglican Church was established there to meet the spiritual needs of the colonists, who were members of the Church of England. About the same time a group of Congregationalists, persecuted in England because of their religious views, took refuge in Holland. Finally they made arrangements with the London Company to settle in Virginia. But the Mayflower and the Pilgrims landed at Plymouth, Massachusetts, instead, introducing Congregationalism to New England in 1620. A decade later the Massachusetts Bay Company came with its charter, stockholders, and board of directors to plant colonies at Salem and Boston. These Puritans sought to escape the despotism of Charles I and to find freedom of worship, but the economic reasons for colonization were much greater than religious historians often have been willing to admit. Like the Pilgrims, the Puritans were Calvinistic in doctrine; and they ultimately also accepted the congregational form of government. In 1691 the Pilgrim and Puritan settlements amalgamated to form Massachusetts.

Meanwhile, because of Puritan intolerance and economic advantage, settlers of a Congregational conviction spilled over into Connecticut on the south and Maine, New Hampshire and Vermont on the north. And separatists such as Roger Williams moved to Rhode Island, where Baptist Churches were first organized on North American shores and where separation of Church and State was practiced in an atmosphere of almost complete religious liberty.

Both Puritans and Anglicans were interested in an educated ministry and founded colleges for that purpose. In 1693 the Anglicans opened William and Mary in Williamsburg. In 1636 and 1701 respectively the Puritans launched Harvard and Yale. Because denser population in towns permitted it, the New Englanders also built elementary and secondary schools to enable the populace to read the Bible and to provide for them other religious instruction.

About the time Massachusetts settlers were spilling over into Connecticut, Lord Baltimore was planting a colony in Maryland. Although Baltimore designed his colony as a haven for persecuted Catholics, not too many came. Therefore, in order to maintain a successful economic venture, he permitted religious toleration. Puritans came in large numbers, but Anglicanism was established at the end of the century when Maryland became a royal colony.

Because Quakers were persecuted both in England and New England, William Penn sought to provide a haven for them in Pennsylvania during the last decades of the seventeenth century. And because Quakerism did not lend itself to exclusiveness and because **Penn** wanted a profitable colony, the doors were thrown open to all who would come. Penn advertised widely in Europe with good success, and Germans came in droves to Penn's Woods. There were Lutherans, Moravians, and a host of German sects. West Jersey, too, became a Quaker settlement.

In 1623 New Amsterdam was founded on Manhattan Island. While the Dutch did not profess any religious motivation for colonization, they naturally favored the Reformed Church, the first one appearing in 1628. New York developed a cosmopolitan character, however, and the efforts of Dutch governors to enforce religious conformity were never successful. After the English took over New Netherland, they established the Anglican Church there in 1693—at least in New York City and surrounding counties. Lutherans settled in New Amsterdam almost as soon as the Dutch Reformed, but they did not fare very well under Dutch rule. The Lutherans were more successful, however, in the Swedish colony on the Delaware, planted in 1638. This too fell into the hands of the Dutch and finally into the hands of the English. The first permanent English Presbyterian church was also established in New Netherland—on Long Island in 1640. But the Presbyterians in the early days were most numerous in East Jersey and Pennsylvania.

THE EIGHTEENTH CENTURY

The development of the colonies south of Virginia came during the eighteenth century, and in all of them the Anglican Church became the established Church. Anglicanism was established in South Carolina in 1706, Georgia in 1758, and North Carolina in 1765. The eighteenth century was also one in which the Anglican Church made a determined effort to reorganize and to improve ministers, morals, and service rendered in the parishes. The famous Society for the Propagation of the Gospel in Foreign Parts took the lead in this effort.

In general, then, it may be said that at the time of the American Revolution the Anglican Church dominated the Southern colonies, the Congregational Church the Northern colonies, while in the middle colonies there was diversity. To be more specific, the Anglican Church was the established church in Georgia, Virginia, North Carolina, South Carolina, Maryland, New York City and surrounding counties. The Congregational Church was established in Massachusetts (Maine), Connecticut and New Hampshire. In New Jersey, Pennsylvania, Delaware, and Rhode Island there was no state Church. It is remarkable that while in the rest of the world before, during, and after the American Revolution a state Church was everywhere established, in the United States complete separation of Church and State was achieved, with the accompanying disestablishment of the Church.

There were several reasons for this. First, the kind and extent of immigration that flowed into the colonies after 1690 was significant. There were Huguenots and Quakers. Then came a great wave of some 200,000 Germans. While a great percentage of these were Lutheran and Reformed, many smaller sects were represented; and of the total most were dominated by the Pietistic emphasis on inner, personal religion. Last came a wave of about 250,000 Scotch-Irish from North Ireland—Presbyterians who were persecuted by the Anglican Church there. They spread widely over the thirteen colonies and contributed greatly to religious diversity. By 1760 there were about 2,500,000 in the colonies, of which about one third were foreign born.

A second influence favoring disestablishment was the effect of the proprietary colonies. All the colonies established after 1660 were proprietary grants. Something has already been said about how the desire for a successful colonial venture led to religious toleration in Pennsylvania, and especially Maryland. The same is true for New York, Georgia, North and South Carolina, New Jersey and Delaware. Third, we should note the leveling influence of the great revivals that shook the colonies during the eighteenth century. The revivals transcended denominational lines, and the revivalists stressed the equality of all men in the sight of God. Fourth, pioneering attitudes made a contribution similar to that of the revivals. The frontier was a leveler. Moreover, the pioneer must become a self-reliant individualist if he is to survive. Individualism and religious institutionalism did not mix well. Fifth, the impact of the unchurched was significant. Because the frontier moved so fast and people were spread out in such a thin line, the churches failed to keep up with the needs of the population. Many were without church membership—in proportion to the population, probably more than anywhere else in Christendom at the time. Unchurched do not have much interest in established religion.

Sixth, natural rights philosophy influenced many. Something was said in the last chapter about natural rights philosophy and the rise of deism during the eighteenth century. One of the rights that educated men of that day came to accept was the privilege of deciding what brand of religious belief they should accept. John Locke in his *Letters on Toleration* (1689–1706) had argued for the separation of church and state and the voluntary nature of one's religious affiliation. Many leaders of the American Revolutionary generation, such as Jefferson, were greatly imbued with this philosophy. Perhaps it is of interest to observe that the state Church was first disestablished in Virginia, where natural rights philosophy was very strong.

Lastly, agitation for the appointment of an Anglican bishop in America, especially on the part of the Society for the Propagation of the Gospel, stirred fires of disestablishment. Cries of dismay rose from the influential Congregational and Presbyterian camps. And coming as it did when the colonists increasingly resented the rule of Parliament, this proposal stirred political opposition as well as religious. If Parliament could establish religion in all the colonies, it could by so much tighten the noose around the necks of a people looking for greater freedom.

Thus it may be seen that disestablishment was almost a foregone conclusion in the United States. With the founding of the new nation, one after another the edifices of state Church establishment toppled. The last to go was Congregationalism: in New Hampshire, 1817; Connecticut, 1818; and Massachusetts, 1833.

If there was so much religious diversity and agitation pro and con during the eighteenth century, it may be well to ask about the attitude of the various denominations toward the Revolution and their part in it. The Anglicans were divided, with a probable loyalist majority. In the North they were generally loyalist; but in the South many of the great planters, among them Washington, favored the Revolutionary Cause. The Congregationalists gave enthusiastic support, their ministers preaching sermons in support of the patriot cause. The Presbyterians were whole-heartedly patriot, their struggle with royal governors and the Anglican Church in the colonies being something of a continuation of the Presbyterian-Episcopalian conflict in England. One of the greatest Presbyterian patriots was John Witherspoon, signer of the Articles of Confederation and the only clergyman to sign the Declaration of Independence. Lutherans also enthusiastically supported the Revolution, especially under the leadership of the Muhlenbergs. Though divided, the Roman Catholics generally were patriot. The Baptists supported the Revolution because, for one thing, they felt that the cause of separation of Church and State was at stake. Methodists were suspect because Wesley at the beginning of the war urged neutrality; but native born preachers seem to have been in sympathy with the Revolution. Although Quakers, Mennonites, and Moravians were conscientious objectors, a large percentage of them were in sympathy with the Revolution and some even joined the army.

The Revolution brought about the dissolution of ties between many religious bodies in America and Europe, necessitating separate organization in America. For other reasons some groups likewise organized. William White and Samuel Seabury, Jr., were responsible for rehabilitating the Anglican Church after the war; and it was organized as the Protestant Episcopal Church in 1789, along more democratic lines than the Church of England. Cut loose from English Methodism by the force of circumstances, the Methodists organized in 1784 as the Methodist Episcopal Church, under the leadership of Francis Asbury. In the same year American Roman Catholic dependence on British jurisdiction terminated, and in 1789 John Carroll became the first Roman Catholic Bishop with Baltimore as his See. The Baptists formed a General Committee in 1784. And the Presbyterians were in Philadelphia drawing up a constitution for their Church at the same time as the national constitution was being formed.

One of the major events of the American Church during the eighteenth century was the Great Awakening. With the loss of evangelical enthusiasm that characterized the first generation of Congregationalists, Presbyterians and others, and with the increase of the unchurched on the expanding frontiers, religion and morals declined all over the colonies. In fact, even the churches were filled with unconverted. To meet such a need came the Great Awakening. The Awakening began with Theodore Frelinghuysen's preaching among the Dutch Reformed of New Jersey in 1726. He in turn influenced the Presbyterian pastors Gilbert and William Tennent, who worked among the Scotch-Irish in the Middle Colonies.

Thence the revival spread to the Congregationalists through the preaching of Jonathan Edwards beginning in 1734. Five years later George Whitefield, associate of the Wesleys, returned to America and preached with tremendous success. He found great outdoor meetings most effective; there were no buildings large enough for the crowds. Whitefield preached in the colonies intermittently until 1769. Ultimately the whole Atlantic seaboard was aflame. Especially during the early days unusual physical manifestations characterized the revival, but in later years this was not generally the case. It should be noted, however, that anxious seats were unknown and inquiry meetings, to which we have become accustomed, were unheard of. Except in rare instances services were confined to Sunday and the mid-week lecture.

Results of the Great Awakening were phenomenal. It is estimated conservatively that about ten per cent of the New England population of some 300,000 was converted; thousands were swept into the Kingdom in the Middle and Southern colonies. There was also a quickening along missionary and educational lines as David Brainerd sought to win the Indians and colleges such as Princeton, King's (Columbia), and Dartmouth were founded to meet the need for ministers of more numerous churches. Moreover, the revival preserved the heritage of the founding fathers and insured its perpetuity amid the desolations of the Revolution.

The war was hard on religious life in America. Because the churches so generally supported the Revolution, the British took out their spite on houses of worship. Pastors and their people were absorbed in the cause of the Revolution, and French deism and atheism were fashionable because of alliance with France. In fact, rationalism took control in the colleges and other intellectual centers of the land. Dark indeed were the closing years of the eighteenth century.

THE NINETEENTH CENTURY

But light was on the way. The Second Evangelical Awakening began in the 1780's. The revival was not characterized by evangelists going to and fro to incite churches to activity. There were few great names connected with it. For the most part services were carried on by the pastors in their respective churches. In New England the revival was quiet, not accompanied by emotional manifestations as during the first awakening. The situation on the frontier was different, however. There the Presbyterians inaugurated the camp meeting to which thousands came from far and near. Emotional outbreaks, such as falling, rolling, or dancing were common in these meetings; but they did not seem to hinder the effect of the revival. The Methodists and Baptists benefited most from the camp meetings. The effects of the revival were tremendous: 1. The colleges of the land were largely reclaimed through the overthrow of infidelity. 2. There was a spiritual quickening of the churches, the Methodists alone gaining some 40,000 members. 3. Lines were more clearly drawn between rationalism and evangelicalism, and there was a split between the Unitarians and evan--

gelicals in the Congregational Church. 4. The midweek prayer meeting and Sunday schools became common features of church life. 5. Close to a score of new colleges and seminaries were founded. 6. Missionary endeavor was spurred. The American Board of Commissioners for Foreign Missions came into being in 1810; one of its first missionaries was Judson. The American Bible Society was founded in 1816, the American Tract Society in 1825.

As the Second Evangelical Awakening began to lose some of its force, Charles G. Finney came on the scene with his revival efforts. Beginning in New York State in 1824, he conducted very effective meetings in Wilmington, Philadelphia, New York City, Rochester, and many other places. Ultimately he became president of Oberlin, where he was a most influential leader. The teachings of Finney and Asa Mahan included entire consecration, sinless perfection in this life, and freedom of the will. Finney also introduced the anxious seat into modern evangelism. Out of the Oberlin School came the Holiness and Pentecostal Churches. Not only did Finney's work shake America, but he also made two trips to Europe where he experienced extensive revival.

Another revival spread across the North in 1857. Jeremiah Lanphier instituted noon prayer meetings at North Dutch Church in New York. Soon the city was moved as other Churches held similar meetings. The meetings spread to Philadelphia, Albany, Boston, Chicago, and other large cities. It is estimated that there were at least 500,000 conversions in the United States. In 1859 the influence of this revival spread to the British Isles. During the Civil War a revival began among the Confederate forces around Richmond in 1861 and became a general moving of the Spirit by 1863. Perhaps 150,000 or more were converted in this revival.

One of the greatest of modern revivalists was D. L. Moody, whose preaching was of the old evangelical type, a middle of the road Calvinism, rather than the Arminian approach of the Finney and the Holiness preaching of the century. He urged predominately the love of God as the great reason for repentance. Starting out in the YMCA and army camps during the Civil War, he conducted mass evangelism campaigns with the assistance of Ira D. Sankey in the large cities during the last three decades of the century. Not only did he have remarkable success in this country but made several trips to England, one of the most notable of which was the 1873-75 campaign during which he preached to over 2,500,000 in London alone. One of his better known accomplishments was the founding of the Moody Bible Institute. R. A. Torrey, J. Wilbur Chapman and other evangelists followed. And revivalism has been a continuing characteristic of American Christianity.

While revivalism was one very important feature of the nineteenth century, division and reunification of the Churches was another. As a result of agitation over the slavery issue and dissolution of the Union, many denominations split: the Methodists in 1844, the Baptists in 1845, the Presbyterians in 1858 and 1861, and the Lutherans in 1863. The period following the War marked the efforts of the Churches to unite once more.

During and after the War the Churches became more alert to their social obligations. City rescue missions, orphanages, hospitals, homes for the aged and other agencies were established to meet the needs of various groups. The YMCA and YWCA movements spread rapidly across the country to meet the need of youth in the cities for lodging, social activity, and Bible study. This social concern has become more pronounced in the twentieth century.

In addition to the slavery issue, rationalism or liberalism also disturbed the American Church scene during the century. As has been noted, the Unitarian defection greatly reduced the ranks of the Congregational Church early in the century. But especially during the last quarter of the century liberalistic ideas were imported from Germany and England. The Tubingen and Wellhausen schools of thought in Germany, as interpreted by such English scholars as S. R. Driver drew an especially large following. This departure from conservative theology was to become more pronounced during the twentieth century, when it gave rise to the fundamentalist-modernist controversy.

At the end of the century, too, a large number of faith missions came into existence for the propagation of the gospel on foreign fields. A few of them include: Africa Inland Mission, 1895; Central American Mission, 1890; Evangelical Alliance, 1890; The Regions Beyond Missionary Union, 1878; Sudan Interior Mission, 1901.

While evangelical Christianity demonstrated greater concern about propagating the message, other groups that differed to a greater or lesser degree appeared on the American religious scene. The Mormon movement came into being in 1830, the Seventh-Day Adventists in the following year, Spiritualism in 1848, and Christian Science in 1876.

American Christianity has been characterized by full religious freedom, the separation of Church and State, the voluntary principle of Church membership, a democratic approach both in government and lay participation, a high degree of informality in worship services and a tendency toward the multiplication of denominations and sects.

Chapter IX

THE PRESENT SITUATION

How do we stand 2,000 years after Christ delivered the Great Commission? True Christianity is fighting for its life. It seems strange to make such an allegation when over sixty percent of the American people are church members and the percentage continues to climb; when Billy Graham can report such tremendous meetings in the United States, England, Scotland, and Australia; when the sale of Russell Hitt's *Jungle Pilot* (biography of Nate Saint, one of the five martyrs in Ecuador) totaled over 35,000 copies before publication date. Yet it is true that Christianity is fighting for its life.

The external forces contending with Evangelical Christianity are at least fourfold: Communism, nationalism and national or pagan religions, Catholicism, and the cults.

Karl Marx formulated his economic, political and religious philosophy about the middle of the last century as an antidote to a rampant capitalism. He appealed to the down-trodden workers in industrial nations to throw off the bondage with which they were yoked and to introduce a new classless society. But in the industrial nations the lot of the worker slowly improved through the efforts of labor unions, governmental intervention, and the great reformers. So it was in the agrarian nation of Russia that Communism, as reconstructed or reinterpreted by Lenin, first caught fire. Now it has engulfed over 800 millions of people and knocks at the door of India, Southeast Asia, and various countries of the Middle East, Latin America, and Europe. Wherever it has gone this

atheistic system has sought utterly to uproot Christianity
—either by direct onslaught or subversion. While Communism has not been able to obliterate Christianity in
the countries where it has won control, it has surely
proved to be a formidable enemy.

Nationalism and national religions also vie with Christianity for the mastery. Where nationalistic movements
have resulted in the creation of new states, the religious
body with the largest number of adherents has tended to
assume leadership and establish a state religion. Moslems
predominate in Pakistan and Indonesia, Hindus in India,
and Buddhists in Burma. Therefore Christian work does
not enjoy the freedom which existed under friendly British or Dutch governments. Moreover, in many countries
Christianity has been linked in the minds of the people
with Western imperialism. Now that those countries have
cut the cord which binds them to a foreign power, they
find it hard to accept the religion of that power. And
strongly nationalistic peoples do not care to be evangelized from abroad; such activity puts them on an inferior level.

The religio-political system of Roman Catholicism
also poses as a threat to evangelical Christianity. In city
after city of the United States it has been successful in
filling public offices with its candidates. In New England
the population is two-fifths Catholic, one-fifth Protestant,
and two-fifths unchurched. In Holland, a traditionally
Calvinistic country, the balance has been slowly swinging
to the Catholics. Of the approximately ten million in the
country, about four million are Protestant, about four
million are Catholic, and about two million unchurched.
In Germany, with a large percentage of the Protestant
area swept behind the Iron Curtain, the balance of power
has swung to the Catholics. In Northern Ireland the
number of Catholics has been increasing rapidly; within

the foreseeable future they may be able to win an election in favor of union with Eire. Wherever Romanism has been able to take control, she has persecuted those who differed. Witness the persecutions in Colombia in recent years. It should be noted, however, that in many nations of the world, especially in Latin America, liberal ideas have influenced governments to the point of allowing Protestants greater liberties. And the growth of Protestants in Latin America has been great, especially in Brazil.

Yet another threat to evangelical Christianity is the cults. Especially is this true in the United States. Russellism or Jehovah's Witnesses spreads rapidly among the unsophisticated while Christian Science makes an appeal to the more sophisticated. Mormonism is gaining tremendous power in certain states of the Northwest.

So much for the external forces which Protestant Christianity has to meet today. Now what is going on within Protestantism? To begin with, there has been a basic change in outlook. During the latter part of the nineteenth century and the early part of the twentieth, optimism pervaded the Church. In liberal circles this was expressed in terms of the perfectability of human nature and the idea that man actually was improving. Ultimately a utopian state would be reached. The Darwinian concept of evolution and the striking number of new inventions that promised a better future life for mankind gave credence to that view. In more conservative circles this optimism was expressed in terms of post-millennialism, according to which it was thought that the Gospel would pervade all of society and bring in a reign of righteousness on earth. Two world wars, a devastating depression, German inhumanity toward the Jews, widespread purges of dissenters by the Communists in lands taken over, and a world divided between two powers engaged in a nuclear arms race have virtually annihilated the old utopian or millennial dreams and the concept of perfectability of human nature. Increasingly man is viewed as being incurably bad. Pessimism has become the creed of the day in many circles. Oswald Spengler's *Decline of the West,* written in 1918, expresses this new pessimism.

With the change from optimism to pessimism or realism has come a change in attitude toward the Bible. As a result of archaeological and historical study, it has become increasingly clear to scholars and laymen that the Bible is an essentially accurate historical document. The views of such higher critical schools as Wellhausen and Tubingen moderated greatly. In fact, liberalism in general has become more moderate in attitude toward the Scripture.

As the old optimism died and as the old liberalism moderated, it also became clear that the anti-supernaturalism of previous generations was inadequate for a day when the very foundations of society seemed to be quivering. Some churchmen said, "We have removed the supernatural from the Bible; we have humanized the person of Christ; we have emptied the churches—now what?" The answer seemed to be Neo-Orthodoxy. Led by Karl Barth and Emil Brunner, Neo-Orthodoxy provided a *via media* between the old conservatism and the old liberalism. While holding on to some of the higher critical views of Scripture on the one hand, it stressed on the other hand a supernaturalism, the virgin birth, a sinful humanity who needed salvation; and many of them spoke of the substitutionary death of Christ. Because Neo-Orthodoxy pours new meanings into terms dear to conservatives and because the system has much to say about the Bible *containing* the Word of God and *becoming* the Word of God, it is hard to evaluate. In other words, their view of the Scripture is not a fixed one; a portion of Scripture is inspired as it speaks to a reader on a given day. Neo-Orthodoxy has nearly taken over Protestant Europe, and it is making a determined bid for control of American theological schools. It has become a major foe of the old evangelicalism.

Another characteristic of Christianity today is the ecumenical or union movement. Many means of inter-denominational cooperation were found in the nineteenth century—note for instance the YMCA, organized in 1844. But the twentieth century has seen much more emphasis on interdenominational activity. In the United States the Federal Council of the Churches of Christ in America came into existence in 1908; it changed its name to the National Council in 1950 and became a much more comprehensive organization. Conservatives organized the American Council of Churches in 1941 as their answer to the generally liberal minded National Council. Then in 1948, after many years of preparation the World Council of Churches was formed at Amsterdam, with 147 denominations from forty-four countries participating. In addition to interdenominational cooperation, there has also been considerable organic union of churches in recent years. The United Church of Canada came into being in 1925, the Church of South India in 1947, the National Church of Scotland in 1929; the Methodist Church in the United States in 1939; and a host of unions took place in other lands.

Within the great denominations and existing as separatist groups is a significant number of evangelical Christians. This element has become increasingly vocal and respected in recent years. It has benefited greatly from the rehabilitation of the Bible in scholarly circles as a result of Near Eastern studies. An increasing number of evangelicals have trained in the finest universities of the world and now serve as professors and department heads in the universities. Fully accredited Christian colleges dot the American countryside; and an Accrediting Association of Bible Colleges has come into being, with a growing list of fully accredited and associate members. Several religious radio stations have been constructed, and individual programs are aired on national and international hookups. Again mass evangelism is stirring many of the great cities of the world, especially through the efforts of Billy Graham and his team.

But of special encouragement is the effective presentation of the Gospel on foreign fields. As a result of the indigenous program, self-supporting churches are springing up all over the world; and when nationalism no longer permits or makes advisable foreign control of mission work, native churches are often reasonably ready to go on their own. New techniques in missions are speeding the message on its way and making existing work more effective. Missionary radio will soon blanket the globe. Already the list of stations is long; note for example HCJB in Ecuador, ELWA in Liberia, TGNA in Guatemala, CP-27, Bolivia, Far Eastern Broadcasting Station in the Philippines, and the Voice of Tangier in North Africa. Missionary aviation is coming into its own. Missionary Aviation Fellowship was organized in 1944, and a large number of other organizations use planes in their work. The Moody Bible Institute has instituted the missionary technical course with majors in aviation and radio. Gospel recordings and colportage work are used extensively. Religious journalism is a new hope for Christian evangelism. The *Envol* publications make their way in the Congo, *Africa Challenge* and *Our Africa* elsewhere in Africa, and *Dengta* in Hong Kong. The Wycliffe Bible Translators is a new type of missionary agency, founded in 1933, and dedicated to the task of reducing to writing the languages of approximately two thousand remaining unreached tribes and translating the Bible into those languages.

The picture of aggressive evangelicalism painted in the last few hundred words does not seem to support the statement made at the beginning of this chapter that true Christianity is fighting for its life. But that claim remains valid. Not only does evangelical Christianity today fight Communism, nationalism and pagan religions, Catholicism, and the cults without, but its wars against a deadly secularization and respectability within. In America at least it has become the correct thing to join a church and be seen there, either for the peace of mind or social and economic advance that such an act brings. Unfortunately the Church's influence on the people has not risen appreciably with the growing membership figures. The increase in crime, the divorce rate, alcoholism, and immorality in general demonstrates that the message of the Church is not speaking very eloquently or convincingly to the society of which she is a part. It is time then for the Church, in America at least, to make an agonizing reappraisal. Where do we go from here?

BIBLIOGRAPHY

Rather than list an extensive bibliography or mention a number of primary source works for Church history, it is thought that the reader would profit most from a select list of general works readily available in libraries and book stores. The present work has been very limited in space; therefore emphasis has been on the West: Roman Catholicism and Protestantism. The following will provide more detail on the East (including Eastern Europe and the Orient and the Eastern Orthodox Church), as well as filling in the gaps in the present work.

Bainton, R. H., *The Reformation of the Sixteenth Century* (Boston: The Beacon Press, 1952).

Bettenson, Henry, ed., *Documents of the Christian Church* (New York: Oxford University Press, 1947).

Cairns, Earle E., *Christianity Through the Centuries* (Grand Rapids: Zondervan Publishing House, 1954).

Grimm, Harold J., *The Reformation Era* (New York: The Macmillan Company, 1954).

Klotsche, E. H. and Mueller, J. T., *The History of Doctrine* (Burlington, Iowa: The Lutheran Literary Board, 1945).

Latourette, Kenneth S., *A History of Christianity* (New York: Harper and Brothers, 1953).

Mead, Frank S., *Handbook of Denominations in the United States* (New York: Abingdon Press, 1956).

Neve, D. L., *A History of Christian Thought,* 2 vols. (Philadelphia: The Muhlenberg Press, 1946).

Newman, Albert H., *A Manual of Church History,* 2 vols. (Philadelphia: American Baptist Publication Society, 1931).

Qualben, Lars P., *A History of the Christian Church* (New York: Thomas Nelson & Sons, 1942).

Renwick, A. M., *The Story of the Church* (Grand Rapids: Wm. B. Eerdmans Publishing Co., 1958).

Schaff, Philip, *History of the Christian Church,* 7 vols. (New York: Charles Schribner's Sons, 1910). Reprinted by Wm. B. Eerdmans Publishing Co.

Sweet, William W., *The Story of Religion in America* (New York: Harper and Brothers, rev. ed., 1950).

Walker, Williston, *A History of the Christian Church* (New York: Charles Scribner's Sons, rev. ed., 1959).